AMINATA COOTE

Forgive Them

21 Devotions on Forgiveness

Contents

Introduction

Dear friend,

Thank you for purchasing this devotional on forgiveness. I'm not an expert on this topic, but someone desiring to learn more about forgiveness, so I can live it out in my daily life.

I wish there was no need for us to learn forgiveness. That people never hurt our feelings or we never became angry or did foolish things.

Sadly, offending others is a part of life—people treat us carelessly and we do the same to others.

Perhaps you have different reasons for wanting to learn forgiveness. Maybe there's one person who did something so heinous, and you're trying to make sense of it. You know you need to forgive this person, but it's hard!

Why did God ask us to forgive those who trample on our feelings or hurt us?

The Oxford Online Dictionary defines forgive in the following ways:

- stop feeling angry or resentful towards (someone) for an offence, flaw, or mistake.
- no longer feel angry about or wish to punish (an offence, flaw, or mistake).
- cancel (a debt).

To fully embrace the biblical definition of forgiveness, we must do all the above. We must let go of our desire to see the person punished. We must release our resentment and pain to find healing and peace.

Finally, it's imperative to cancel that person's debt, releasing our desire for revenge or retribution.

It sounds easier than it is. Yet, this is what Christ requires: for us to forgive each other as He forgave us.

To be clear, forgiveness does not mean giving the person the opportunity to hurt you again. Sometimes, forgiveness includes restoration or distancing ourselves from those who routinely hurt and degrade us.

Let us walk through 21 stories of forgiveness in the Bible to unlock this powerful skill. We'll learn how to release grouses and be more Christ-like, which should be every Christian's goal.

I'm praying for you, sweet friend. May you find freedom as you forgive those who have wronged you. May the peace of God guard your heart and mind.

Your partner along the journey,

Aminata

I

Devotionals

1

God Forgives You When You Fail

Proverbs 28:13 NKJV — He who covers his sins will not prosper, But whoever confesses and forsakes them will have mercy.

"*D*arling?" *Adam wandered through the garden, searching for his wife. She had been beside him until he'd gotten distracted watching the lion cubs play.*

He inhaled the fragrant air, enjoying the warm sun on his skin.

"Thank You for another beautiful day, Father." He lifted his face toward heaven, certain Jehovah watched him with delight and received his praise.

"Sweetheart?" Adam went deeper into the garden. His bride wasn't in any of her favorite places. He'd checked.

Instinct had him creeping closer to the center of the garden. But why would she be there?

The only things in the center were the Trees of Life and Of Knowledge of Good and Evil.

He quickened his footsteps. Adam froze when he spotted his bride under the forbidden tree with one of its fruit in her hand. No!

Surely she hadn't eaten from the tree. For God said if either of them ate it, they'd die. He wasn't sure what that meant, but the way God said it convinced Adam it wasn't something he wanted.

"There you are!" His lips spread into a wide smile and he hurried to her side.

"Oh, Adam." She gazed up at him, her eyes filled with wonder. "You must try this. It's delicious."

She held out the fruit and he recoiled.

"No!"

His bride chuckled, her shoulders shaking with laughter. "It won't bite you, silly. Doesn't it look good?"

It looked tasty. Its purple skin glistened where the light hit it. A sweet fragrance, such as he'd never smelled before, emanated from it, and his mouth watered.

"God commanded us not to eat from the forbidden tree."

Plants were abundant in the garden, and this was the only one restricted from them.

"God." His wife scoffed, her lips curled in an expression he'd never seen before. "What does He know?" She leaned forward, a conspiratorial gleam in her eyes. "I know things—wonderful things. The serpent said this would make me like God and he was right."

She threw her head back, laughing with glee.

Serpent? Was she joking when she said it talked to her? He ran his gaze over his beautiful bride. The only change was this boldness that he kinda liked.

"Come on, sweetie," she cajoled, waving the produce before his nose.

His stomach rumbled, anticipating the sweet juice hitting his tongue.

"Alright." He closed his eyes and took a bite.

* * *

The first couple's fall is a familiar story. They had plenty of food to eat, but disobeyed God, partaking in the one item He withheld.

While Adam and Eve didn't die immediately, humanity and the entire universe are paying the penalties for their sin.

Let's look at some consequences:

The couple experienced shame and fear for the first time. Before the Fall, the man and woman were naked and unashamed (Genesis 2:25).

Before their transgression, they communed with God and had no reason to be afraid of Him (Genesis 3:8-10). Afterward, they could no longer stand in His presence.

The serpent became "cursed above all cattle", relegated to a life on its stomach, eating the dust of the earth (Genesis 3:14).

Conception and childbirth became painful for the woman. She also lost her equality in dominion and became submissive to her husband (Genesis 3:16).

The ground became cursed, producing thistles and thorns and requiring hard labor to reap its crops (Genesis 3:17-19).

Animals died to provide clothing, and possibly a sacrifice for their transgression (Genesis 3:21).

God banished them from the garden and the couple lost their home (Genesis 3:22-24).

Today, we're still reaping the consequences of sin. Hardship, hatred, sickness, war, and crime illustrate the effects of sin on humanity.

But I'm glad God didn't abandon us to fend for ourselves. Along with the punishment, there was a promise that things wouldn't remain dire.

Genesis 3:15 NKJV — "And I will put enmity Between you

and the woman, And between your seed and her Seed; He shall bruise your head, And you shall bruise His heel."

Sin separated humanity from God, putting an impassable barrier between us. But the plan of salvation made it possible for us to be restored to a position of blamelessness before Him.

God could have destroyed the first couple, along with our universe and everything in it. He could have wiped the slate clean and started fresh.

Instead, He offered our forefathers grace. He made a way for them to be restored. He sent His precious Son to pay the death penalty.

My friend, if God forgave Adam and Eve, He'll also forgive you when you ask.

The enemy excels at convincing us that our sins are too great to be forgiven. Just as he lied in the Garden of Eden, he does the same now.

Do not be like Eve, who believed the devil rather than her heavenly Father. Confess your sins and accept restoration and healing.

Prayer

Abba,

Sometimes the enemy's lies are tempting. It seems easier to do wrong than to live up to Your standards.

I know that's a lie. The enemy comes to kill, steal, and destroy. He doesn't want me living my best life. Help me resist his enticing lies and do what You've commanded me to.

Thanks for Your willingness to forgive and abundance of grace. In Jesus' name, Amen.

Go Deeper

Read Genesis 2-3

- Imagine what life may have been like in Eden. Why do you think Eve listened to (and obeyed) the serpent?
- Compare Eve's response to your own. How often do you disobey God, choosing an alternative because it seems easier or faster (or whatever adjective fits)?
- What lessons can you learn from this account and how might you implement them?

Key Points

1. Adam and Eve disobeyed God by eating the forbidden fruit, leading to spiritual separation from Him.
2. Their sin introduced shame, fear, suffering, and death into the world, affecting humanity and creation.
3. Despite their failure, God offered grace, promising salvation through the woman's offspring, who would ultimately defeat the serpent.

2

Forgiveness Requires Time

Ephesians 4:31 NKJV — Let all bitterness, wrath, anger, clamor, and evil speaking be put away from you, with all malice.

Rebekah's stomach churned. What was going on? It had been like this for days—weeks. Her stomach twisting as if her insides were at war.

She lay prostrate on the ground. "Heavenly Father, what is happening? Am I dying?"

She trembled as she waited for the answer. She didn't want to die. Life was good, and her husband Isaac was a good man.

Though she hadn't given him children, she had a wonderful life. She mourned for her barren womb. Why wasn't she able to bear children? Isaac had prayed for her and still her womb remained empty.

"Two nations are in thy womb, and two manner of people shall be separated from thy bowels."

She sat up as the Lord's voice echoed through her spirit. She was pregnant? Her hands fluttered to rest against her stomach.

"And the one people shall be stronger than the other people," the

8

Lord continued, "and the elder shall serve the younger."

She was pregnant. With twins! Tears of thanksgiving streamed down her cheeks.

Praise the Lord!

* * *

The brothers animosity started in the womb. Their mother, Rebekah, had such a difficult pregnancy that she asked God what was going on. That's when she found out she was having twins!

After being barren for twenty years, she would have two sons.

It's natural for siblings to squabble, but there was something unusual about the twin's rivalry. The younger came out of the womb grasping Esau's foot.

And so it was with their relationship—Jacob envied Esau and schemed to achieve what he had.

Two pivotal moments in the twins' relationship set the course for the rest of their lives.

The first was the day Esau came home from the field, famished. Jacob was cooking a pot of lentils, and, in response to Esau's request, offered to trade a bowl of soup for the birthright.

To put things into perspective, the birthright was an honor. It represented the firstborn's right to inherit the father's estate and become the family's next patriarch.

The firstborn also received a double portion of the inheritance.

Though they were born on the same day, Jacob knew his place. He was the second-born and would receive a smaller share of his father's assets. But that wasn't enough for him. He wanted more.

Esau's hunger made him shortsighted, valuing immediate

gratification over long-term blessings.

Genesis 25:32 NLT — "Look, I'm dying of starvation!"
said Esau. "What good is my birthright to me now?"

They completed the trade, and Esau sold his birthright for a bowl of stew.

The second event happened when Isaac was old and sightless. Determined to bless his older son before he died, Isaac called Esau and requested a special meal.

Sadly, his wife intercepted the message. Rebekah encouraged Jacob to steal Esau's blessing and helped him enact the plan.

Isaac's blessing was powerful—making Jacob the leader of their family and blessing him with prosperity and wealth.

When Esau returned from the hunt, his father had nothing left for him but the paltry promise that one day he'd break the yoke of his brother's dominance.

Anger and hatred grew in Esau's heart. Twice, his younger brother had stolen from him. Twice, he'd lost something valuable through Jacob's schemes.

Esau pledged to kill his younger brother as soon as their father was dead.

Jacob's death would solve many problems for Esau. He'd receive the entire inheritance and avenge himself for his younger brother's treachery.

But it was not to be, as once again his mother intervened. Jacob went to their relatives in Paddan Aram and Esau didn't see his twin for twenty years.

Did he receive news about his brother? It seems unlikely, as Esau appeared surprised to see Jacob's family when they reunited (Genesis 33:5).

Can you imagine what Esau went through in those twenty years?

Had he learned of his mother's role in Jacob's deception? Did he forgive her before she died? Perhaps he wrestled with his anger for years, struggling to let go of the pain his brother and mother caused.

Did Esau wonder how his brother fared away from home? Did he even know if Jacob got to their relatives safely?

After Jacob left, Esau married Mahalath, his third wife. He and his wives had children. He hunted and provided for his family. One day, he received a messenger who claimed Jacob was on his way home.

The Bible tells us nothing about Esau's interim years, but the man who wept on his brother's shoulder was not the man who plotted to kill him twenty years earlier.

While Scripture doesn't document why Esau forgave Jacob, this account has two important lessons.

1. Forgiveness may take time. It would be wonderful if we forgave every offense against us the second it happened. And for some things we do.

Some transgressions require time to process the pain and wrestle with God about our feelings.

2. Forgiveness sometimes requires distance.

Depending on the transgression, it might be hard to be around the person as we work on forgiving them. This is especially true if they're not repentant.

My friend, forgiveness may be difficult, but it's not impossible when we access the power of Christ in us to forgive.

Prayer

Dear heavenly Father,

Sometimes I struggle to forgive those who hurt me. Please help me forgive because their offenses are pitiable compared to my sins.

Give me the time and space I need to forgive, for I ask it in Jesus' name, Amen.

Go Deeper

Read Genesis 25:19-34 and Genesis 27-33

- Imagine yourself in Esau's position. How do you think he felt after his brother stole the two things that belonged to him as the firstborn?
- What do you believe softened Esau's heart in the intervening years?
- Imagine yourself in Jacob's position. Do you think he was repentant when he met Esau after a twenty-year absence? What do you believe may have influenced his change of heart?
- Is there someone who wronged you in a way that was life-changing? Begin the hard work of forgiving that person today.

Key Points

1. The story of Esau and Jacob illustrates the emotional and relational consequences of deceit and rivalry.
2. Forgiveness often requires time, space, and God's trans-formative power to soften hearts.
3. Esau's eventual forgiveness reminds us that even the deepest wounds can heal through grace and personal growth.

3

Forgiveness Is Transformative

*Matthew 6:14-15 NKJV — "For if you forgive men their trespasses,
your heavenly Father will also forgive you.
"But if you do not forgive men their trespasses, neither will your
Father forgive your trespasses."*

J *oseph stared at the men kneeling before him. He recognized
them instantly, but, with his changed appearance, he was a
stranger to them.*

*"You're spies!" he accused them. "You're here to see how
vulnerable our land has become."*

*He observed their every expression and body movement. These
men had thrown him into an empty cistern and planned to leave
him there to die. But a band of Ishmaelite traders passed by, and his
brothers sold him into slavery instead.*

Did they ever think about him or regret what they'd done?

*"Your servants are twelve brothers," they replied. "We're the sons
of one man in the land of Canaan, the youngest is with our father
and one is no longer alive."*

That answered one of his questions. How would he know if their transformation was genuine?

"I'll test your story. One of you will go for your younger brother while the others remain in prison."

He ordered their imprisonment and walked away, still uncertain of their character and needing time to discern their true intentions.

It only took three days for him to realize he couldn't keep them in jail. They imprisoned him without cause for years, but keeping his brothers in prison wasn't right.

He faced his brothers, heart heavy with the decision he had to make. "I'm a God-fearing man."

He paused, considering whether his actions would have pleased God. Joseph knew the Lord blessed him when he honorer God.

"Leave one of your brothers behind and bring food to your starving families."

Their response would reveal who they truly were: brothers who competed among themselves and secretly detested each other.

They looked at each other. "Clearly we are being punished because of what we did to Joseph." They spoke in their native tongue, unaware that he understood them.

"We saw his anguish when he pleaded for his life, but we didn't listen. That's why we're in trouble."

"Didn't I tell you not to sin against him?" Reuben asked, glaring at his brothers. "But you didn't listen. And now we must answer for his blood!"

Overcome by emotion, Joseph rushed from the room to weep. He cried for the young boy he'd been—the boy who'd craved his brothers' respect and admiration.

His resolve strengthened. He'd do whatever it took to determine if they were honorable men.

He returned to his brothers and singled out Simeon. Once, Simeon *and Levi killed an entire town because a man raped their sister Dinah. If anyone needed redemption, it was Simeon.*

The famine would last for several more years. Unless they wanted to starve, they'd return. He sent his brothers away, second-guessing his choices. Had he done the right thing?

His certainty ebbed and flowed during the months they were gone. Hadn't their food run out? Was his father alive? Was Benjamin? Had something happened to his brothers on their way home? Was that why they hadn't returned?

He almost stumbled over his feet when the messenger told him his brothers were among those who came to buy grain. He spied on them, a fist tightening around his heart when he spotted Benjamin. His little brother was a man now.

Joseph had missed his younger brother's entire life. Was he married? Did he have children? The urge to weep was strong, but he resisted.

He had a plan to execute. His brothers would not leave this time until he knew what manner of men they were.

* * *

Joseph had several reasons to hate his brothers.

1. They despised him because he was Jacob's favored son.
2. They sold him into slavery, depriving him of his family.
3. While he was a slave in Potiphar's house, his mistress accused him of rape and his master imprisoned him. He spent several years in jail.

Joseph could have dwelled on his brothers' treachery, on how their envy reduced him from the favored son of a wealthy man to a slave and then a prisoner.

But Joseph also had reasons to wonder if being sold into slavery had been a necessary part of his journey.

He learned to work hard and persevere through trials. In Egypt, he was no longer Jacob's precious son, shielded from hardship and adversity. He was a slave, subject to his master's whims.

He became closer to God, learning to depend on Him and to act in ways that honored the Lord.

When Joseph saw his brothers again, he would have realized God used him to interpret Pharaoh's dream and save Egypt from the famine.

As Egypt's governor, he could offer sanctuary to his family and save them from famine and financial ruin.

Maybe someone has hurt you, and you're struggling to recover. You don't see how you can forgive them—not when you're angry and hurt. Not when they haven't expressed an ounce of remorse.

My friend, I don't know who you're struggling to forgive, but I encourage you to embark on the challenging journey toward forgiveness. Forgiveness benefits us as much as, if not more, than the one who transgressed against us.

We forgive because God has forgiven us. When we compare our sins against God to what others have done to us, it reveals how merciful God is. If He can forgive us, shouldn't we also forgive others?

Don't let hate and unforgiveness damage your relationship with God.

Prayer

Dear heavenly Father,

I struggle to forgive. Please give me a heart like Yours so I can forgive those who hurt me—even if they never ask for forgiveness or apologize, give me the ability to forgive them.

I release them into Your hands, Lord. Give me peace about what they've done to me. In Jesus' name, Amen.

Go Deeper

Read Genesis 37-50

- Imagine yourself in Joseph's brothers' shoes. What reasons did they have to hate him? Were they justified in their hatred?
- Now, imagine yourself in Joseph's position. How do you think he felt to be hated by most of his siblings? Was there anything he could have done to minimize their envy?
- Consider the impact envy has on a relationship.
- What lessons can you learn about forgiveness from the story of Joseph and his brothers?

Key Points

1. Joseph faced the difficulty of deciding whether his brothers had genuinely changed since their betrayal of him years earlier. Through a series of tests, he sought to understand their hearts and intentions.
2. Joseph's story reveals the importance of forgiveness, even when the offender has not expressed remorse. Forgiveness reflects God's mercy and brings peace to the one offering it.
3. Consider your struggles with forgiveness and its parallels to Joseph's journey. Learn to forgive, even when it seems difficult or undeserved.

4

God's Grace Redeems Your Past

Luke 6:37 NKJV — "Judge not, and you shall not be judged. Condemn not, and you shall not be condemned. Forgive, and you will be forgiven."

R*ahab gazed into the loving eyes of her husband, Salmon. Their families and his entire tribe gathered around them to witness the couple saying their vows.*

She swiped a tear that trekked down her cheek, amazed that this wonderful man had taken a chance on her. That he'd forgiven her.

Not so long ago, she lived in Jericho, plying a trade almost as old as time. She'd been a prostitute, and memories of her old life still stung. But God had forgiven her, and now the only thing left to do was forgive herself.

Her journey toward redemption began the day she hid two Israelite spies. She immediately recognized that the men were different and hid them under the flax stalks on her roof.

And just in time. The king's men came almost immediately, demanding that she turn the men over to them. Fear had ripped at her throat, but how could she turn over those innocent men when

20

she knew it was wrong?

They heard how the Israelite God had destroyed Egypt, killing every firstborn, including Pharaoh's son.

They heard about how the Israelites had defeated the kings of Og and Sihon. How their God had parted the Red Sea for the Israelites to cross on dry land.

Which Canaanite god had such power? Which of them could do such marvelous things?

None that she'd ever seen in all her years. She wasn't putting her faith in gods who'd proven to be deaf, blind, and dumb. Not anymore.

She made up a story to deflect the king's men. After they left, she made a bargain with the spies. They would spare her life because she'd protected them. They'd also save her family.

To her surprise, they'd agreed. Her task was to leave a scarlet cord in her window, keep their secret, and convince her entire family to move into her house.

The first two things were simple enough, but convincing her family...that had taken work.

But with the Israelite God's help, she'd done it, and now she was here—standing amidst her new tribe. No longer a prostitute, a woman outcast from her society, but a bride. A woman redeemed and loved by the Great King.

* * *

The story of Rahab offers hope for anyone who's sinned against God. Her peers couldn't see past her sin—she was always Rahab, the prostitute. Never just Rahab. Or Rahab, the daughter of So-and-So. Not Rahab, who lived along the wall of Jericho. A prostitute.

Yet, God saw value in the redeemed prostitute and incorporated her into the lineage of His Son.

Matthew 1:5 NKJV — Salmon begot Boaz by Rahab, *Boaz begot Obed by Ruth, Obed begot Jesse, (emphasis mine).*

The author of Hebrews talks about her faith.

Hebrews 11:31 NKJV — By faith the harlot Rahab did not perish with those who did not believe, when she had received the spies with peace.

There are some sins people remember forever. Maybe you've experienced this. You made a mistake, said something you shouldn't have, or lived in a way others found shameful.

Years after you've changed, made restitution and moved on with your life, some people won't let you forget it.

They remind you of what you did. They study you with suspicion, expecting you to behave as you did in the past. There's no grace.

Praise the Lord that He is not like us. This is how God treats the repentant:

Isaiah 1:18 NKJV — "Come now, and let us reason together," Says the LORD, "Though your sins are like scarlet, They shall be as white as snow; Though they are red like crimson, They shall be as wool."

Isaiah 43:25 NKJV — "I, even I, am He who blots out your transgressions for My own sake; And I will not remember your sins."

*Psalm 103:12 NKJV — As far as the east is from the west,
So far has He removed our transgressions from us.*

Romans 8:1 NKJV — There is therefore now no condemnation to those who are in Christ Jesus, who do not walk according to the flesh, but according to the Spirit.

My friend, your past may create a pang of shame when you remember, and the enemy loves to remind you of it. But God has promised to blot out your transgressions.

He has wiped the slate clean and given you a new life covered in the righteousness of His Son.

Accept God's grace, which is freely given. And if you haven't asked, take a moment to do so now. Ask God to forgive you and show you the way forward.

Prayer

Dear heavenly Father,

Sometimes I don't feel forgiven. Please help me accept the grace that You've lavished on me. Please reveal any unconfessed sin, so I might seek forgiveness. In Jesus' name, Amen.

Go Deeper

Read Joshua 2, 6, Matthew 1:5

- Imagine yourself as Rahab. How would you convince your family to trust the word of a prostitute?

- How do you think Rahab felt as she waited for the Israelites to attack?
- Why do you believe she's in the genealogy of faith? What does that teach you about God?

Key Points

1. God forgives Rahab, once a prostitute in Jericho, and incorporates her into His greater plan. Her faith and action in protecting the Israelite spies lead to her inclusion in the lineage of Jesus Christ.
2. Despite societal judgment, God forgives the repentant. His grace is unconditional, and He promises to blot out the sins of those who truly turn to Him in faith.
3. Accept God's forgiveness and reflect on your past. Understand that God forgets sins and you can walk in freedom.

5

Forgiveness in the Face of Betrayal

Mark 11:25 NLT — "But when you are praying, first forgive anyone you are holding a grudge against, so that your Father in heaven will forgive your sins, too."

David surveyed the camp opposite the hill where he hid with Abishai. How had his life come to this?

A few short years ago, life had been wonderful. He had been a commander in King Saul's army, going on campaigns against the Philistines, the enemies of his God.

He married Michal, Saul's daughter, and spent time with his best friend, Jonathan. He played music to soothe his lord when the evil spirit tormented Saul. David never would have expected his father-in-law and king to try to kill him.

The first time, he'd been playing to soothe Saul after one of his episodes. He'd excused his king, thinking it was the influence of the evil spirit. But it kept happening—again and again.

One night, Saul sent men to David's house to kill him. If Michal hadn't helped him escape, he'd be dead. Now he'd been on the run for years, living in caves like an animal.

David drew in a breath. It was easy to become angry at Saul, to hate him because of what he'd done.

He tightened his grip on the spear that he'd taken from the king. This was the second time the Lord had delivered Saul into his hands.

Though his men encouraged him, David couldn't bring himself to kill the king. Saul was David's would-be-assassin, but he was also the Lord's anointed.

The first time, he'd cut off a portion of the king's robe. When he confronted Saul (from a distance, of course, he wasn't foolish), he'd thought that was the end. Yet here he was again—in a standoff against Saul and his army.

He cleared his throat so his voice would project to the camp below. "Wake up, Abner!"

* * *

At a glance, the story of David and Saul doesn't appear to be one of forgiveness. Saul attempted to kill David several times until the younger man went on the run.

Though Samuel had anointed David to be Israel's future king, the throne wouldn't be his as long as Saul lived. For some people, that would have been an incentive to get rid of the king. But not David. He trusted God to remove Saul from the throne in His timing (1 Samuel 26:20).

While David had many opportunities to kill Saul, he didn't. He showed Saul grace, trusting God to judge between them—David even mourned Saul's death (2 Samuel 1).

I believe he felt genuine regret that Saul was dead.

The Bible tells us to love our enemies:

Matthew 5:43-45 NKJV — "You have heard that it was

said, 'You shall love your neighbor and hate your enemy.'

"But I say to you, love your enemies, bless those who curse you, do good to those who hate you, and pray for those who spitefully use you and persecute you,

"that you may be sons of your Father in heaven; for He makes His sun rise on the evil and on the good, and sends rain on the just and on the unjust."

Because of Saul's envy, he became David's enemy. Worldly convention, and David's men, suggests that it was acceptable to treat Saul the way he treated David. But that's not what God wants for us. He holds His people to a higher standard.

He wants us to respond with love when we receive only hate. To pray when people persecute us and bless those who curse us.

God asks us to forgive even those who have done unforgivable things. For then we will glorify our Father in heaven.

Prayer

Dear Lord,

I struggle to forgive those who hurt me, especially when they do it repeatedly. I don't know how to forgive my enemies. Sometimes, I don't want to. But I love You and desire to be obedient, so teach me how to forgive them. In Jesus' name, Amen.

Go Deeper

Read 1 Samuel 17–1 Samuel 26

- What differences can you identify between Saul and David? Are there any similarities?
- How does the men's stance with God affect their relationship with others?
- What lessons can you learn about how to treat one's enemies?

Key Points

1. David faced significant betrayal by King Saul, but despite repeated attempts on his life, David refrained from killing Saul, trusting in God's timing for justice.
2. The Bible teaches that forgiveness, even in the face of injustice or wrongs, is a commandment for believers, exemplified by David's response to Saul.
3. God calls us to love and forgive even those who hate and persecute us, trusting that He will bring justice and healing.

6

Forgiven, But Not Free from Consequences

1 John 1:9 NKJV — If we confess our sins, He is faithful and just to forgive us our sins and to cleanse us from all unrighteousness.

As King David listened to Nathan, he became more incensed at the prophet's story. How dare the rich man kill his neighbor's lamb? Had he no conscience? He had many sheep, whereas the neighbor only had one.

"The man who has done this will die." David trembled with righteous anger. "He shall restore his neighbor's lamb four times because he had no pity."

Nathan met his gaze, his eyes unwavering. "You are the man."

The prophet continued to speak on the Lord's behalf, and the Holy Spirit convicted David. He had sinned against the Lord—not once, but multiple times.

Everything started with Bathsheba. He shouldn't have summoned her, especially after learning she was married. When she told him about her pregnancy, he should have acknowledged his guilt and confessed to Uriah.

He tried several tactics to cover up his sin, but Uriah proved to be more righteous than him.

When Uriah refused to sleep with Bathsheba, David arranged for the captain of his army to have him killed. He lost several soldiers that day.

But that wasn't the worst part. He had sinned against God, and there would be consequences—starting with the death of his son.

* * *

David and Bathsheba's story is a cautionary tale against the seductive power of sin. It's a reminder that sin dulls the conscience and, left unchecked, becomes a slippery slope into more transgressions against God.

Though David repented of his sins and God forgave him (2 Samuel 12:13), there were unavoidable consequences.

1. "From this time on, your family will live by the sword because you have despised me by taking Uriah's wife to be your own" (2 Samuel 12:10 NLT).

2. "This is what the LORD says: Because of what you have done, I will cause your own household to rebel against you. I will give your wives to another man before your very eyes, and he will go to bed with them in public view.

You did it secretly, but I will make this happen to you openly in the sight of all Israel." (2 Samuel 12:11-12 NLT).

3. "Nevertheless, because you have shown utter contempt for the LORD by doing this, your child will die." (2 Samuel 12:14 NLT)

Everything that the prophet foretold came true. David's sons—Amnon, Absalom, and Adonijah—died by the sword (2 Samuel 13:28, 2 Samuel 18:14, 1 Kings 2:24-25).

Absalom slept with David's concubines on the palace roof (2 Samuel 16:22). David and Bathsheba's first son died (2 Samuel 12:18).

My friend, God's forgiveness is available to those who repent of their sins and ask for it. But sin has repercussions. God's desire is for us to follow Jesus' example and live blameless, empowered by the Holy Spirit.

Prayer

Dear Lord,

Forgive me for my sins and cleanse me from unrighteousness. I'm grateful that grace is always greater than sin, but I long to live blameless before You.

Purify me so that I may be holy. In Jesus' name, Amen.

Go Deeper

Read 2 Samuel 11-12

- As you read the account of David and Bathsheba, were there any indicators that urged caution?
- What do you learn about the dangers of sin?
- What other lessons about forgiveness did you discover?

Key Points

1. King David's sin with Bathsheba and his subsequent actions (including the death of Uriah) resulted in severe consequences, as foretold by the prophet Nathan. While David repented, the repercussions were unavoidable, such as the deaths of his sons and the humbling of his concubines.
2. God offers forgiveness to those who truly repent, as seen in David's story. However, sin always carries consequences, and while God forgives us, its effects remain.
3. The story of David and Bathsheba serves as a reminder of how unchecked sin can lead to more transgressions, often affecting others and resulting in lasting damage.

7

God's Matchless Grace

Psalm 103:10 NKJV — He has not dealt with us according to our sins, Nor punished us according to our iniquities.

Aaron sat at the entrance of the Tent of Meeting as he and his sons were ordained as priests to the Lord.

His brother, Moses, had washed and dressed him in the special linen outfits made for them. He'd anointed Aaron and his sons with a special oil.

As part of the ordination, they would remain in the Tabernacle for seven days, which gave Aaron plenty of time to reflect.

How could God choose him, of all people, to be His priest after what Aaron had done?

His memory of the golden calf remained sharp, as if it had happened yesterday.

The people had pledged obedience to Jehovah after He appeared to them on the mountain. They'd been terrified of the Lord and asked Moses to speak to Him on their behalf.

Moses left and was gone for days. Long enough for the people to become restless and approach Aaron, begging him to make them an idol. It was as if they had forgotten Jehovah's first commandment.

But they were insistent and so he relented, requesting their gold earrings.

He melted the gold and created a molten calf. He even arranged a festival for this 'god'—an inanimate object he'd created. The object had none of the majesty or power of the one, true God.

It didn't have the power to forgive. Though Aaron had done exactly what God told the Israelites not to do, God chose him to be a priest.

* * *

Moses had been gone for 40 days (Deuteronomy 9:11-12) when they demanded new gods (Exodus 32:1). A stark contrast to their promise in Exodus 19:8 and 24:3 that they would obey the Lord.

> *Exodus 24:3 NKJV — So Moses came and told the people all the words of the LORD and all the judgments. And all the people answered with one voice and said, "All the words which the LORD has said we will do."*

They listened to the commandments, heard the edict not to create any likeness of God or to serve idols. Yet, a few days without their leader and they reverted to Egyptian practices.

Bible scholars believe Aaron's request for the gold earrings of the men and their families was supposed to be a deterrent.

Aaron may have thought those items too precious to part with, underestimating the sway of their desire for a visible representation of God.

Commentators believe that in order for a golden statue to be fashioned, a mold was created and used.

The Bible tells us that Aaron refined the image with an engraving tool.

> *Exodus 32:4 NKJV — And he received the gold from their hand, and he fashioned it with an engraving tool, and made a molded calf. Then they said, "This is your god, O Israel, that brought you out of the land of Egypt!"*

But when Moses confronted him, Aaron didn't admit his culpability. He blamed the people, claiming they had evil tendencies.

He appealed to Moses, seeking sympathy because his brother had experience dealing with the people. Aaron claimed the calf miraculously came out of the fire.

> *Exodus 32:21-24 NIV — He said to Aaron, "What did these people do to you, that you led them into such great sin?"*
>
> *"Do not be angry, my lord," Aaron answered. "You know how prone these people are to evil.*
>
> *They said to me, 'Make us gods who will go before us. As for this fellow Moses who brought us up out of Egypt, we don't know what has happened to him.'*
>
> *So I told them, 'Whoever has any gold jewelry, take it off.' Then they gave me the gold, and I threw it into the fire, and out came this calf!"*

There is no record of Aaron's repentance or seeking forgiveness for his sin. But the Bible tells us God was angry and wanted to destroy him, and would have if Moses hadn't interceded.

> *Deuteronomy 9:20 KJV — And the LORD was very angry with Aaron to have destroyed him: and I prayed for Aaron*

also the same time.

Even after Aaron's sin, the Lord kept the priesthood in his lineage. In fact, since God is omniscient, He knew Aaron would make an idol and incite the people to worship it when He assigned the priesthood to his lineage.

Sometimes, our transgressions make us believe we are unworthy to fulfill God's purpose for our lives. We believe that we're too filthy to do the work that God has called us to do. This is where forgiveness comes in.

Sweet friend, you are not beyond God's ability to forgive. He knew you would sin when He called you. But He promises grace to the repentant and offers His forgiveness. Accept it and move forward in faith.

Prayer

Abba Father,

Thank You for the grace which takes the filthy rags of my righteousness and replaces it with the unblemished righteousness of Christ.

Forgive me of my sins. In Jesus' name, Amen.

Go Deeper

Read Exodus 32 and Deuteronomy 9:7-21

- What do these accounts teach you about sin?
- What do you learn about God's capacity to forgive?

· What other lessons do you learn about God?

Key Points

1. God knows we would sin before we transgress, yet He offers grace.
2. Forgiveness replaces the filthy rags of our unrighteousness and replaces it with Christ's righteousness.
3. You are not beyond God's ability to forgive.

8

God Forgives All Who Repent

Ephesians 1:7 NKJV — In Him we have redemption through His blood, the forgiveness of sins, according to the riches of His grace

T*he mocking cheers of the crowd filled Samson's ears as he performed for them. How had his life come to this?*

Once, he'd been a great judge for his people, the strongest man alive. It started when an angel appeared to his mother.

Before him, his mother had been barren and despaired of ever having children. One day while she was alone, an angel told her she would have a son. The child was to be a Nazirite from the womb and she should avoid strong drink and unclean foods. She was not to shave his head.

All his life, he remained a Nazirite until Delilah. He sighed deeply as he remembered his mistakes.

Why had he thought a prostitute from Gaza would safeguard his secret? Especially after she'd proven fickle? He'd told her fake reasons for his strength and every time she tested him.

His shoulders slumped as he admitted the truth. Deep down, he hoped she would still love him, even if he wasn't the champion people spoke about.

He'd been terribly wrong. Delilah had betrayed him to his enemies, who gouged out his eyes and put him in a prison and compelled him to grind grain. Degrading work. But he deserved it. He'd broken his vow to God, so why shouldn't God punish him?

Now, he was a slave—a trained monkey. One incapable of leading himself.

"Please," he implored the young man who led him. "Place my hands against the pillars that hold up the temple. I want to lean against them to rest."

He allowed the boy to lead him, ashamed at how he'd treated the Almighty God. He'd turned his back on the one true God to become a curiosity in the temple of an idol. But perhaps he could do something to bring glory to the Almighty.

"O Sovereign Lord, please remember me and strengthen me once again."

* * *

The story of Samson is a sad tale about the destructive power of intemperance. His parents dedicated him to the Lord before his birth and there was a certain behavior expected as a Nazirite.

> *Numbers 6:1–9 NLT — Then the Lord said to Moses,*
> *"Give the following instructions to the people of Israel.*
> *"If any of the people, either men or women, take the special vow of a Nazirite, setting themselves apart to the Lord in a special way,*
> *"they must give up wine and other alcoholic drinks. They must not use vinegar made from wine or from other*

alcoholic drinks, they must not drink fresh grape juice, and they must not eat grapes or raisins.

"As long as they are bound by their Nazirite vow, they are not allowed to eat or drink anything that comes from a grapevine—not even the grape seeds or skins.

"They must never cut their hair throughout the time of their vow, for they are holy and set apart to the Lord. Until the time of their vow has been fulfilled, they must let their hair grow long.

"And they must not go near a dead body during the entire period of their vow to the Lord.

"Even if the dead person is their own father, mother, brother, or sister, they must not defile themselves, for the hair on their head is the symbol of their separation to God.

"This requirement applies as long as they are set apart to the Lord.

"If someone falls dead beside them, the hair they have dedicated will be defiled. They must wait for seven days and then shave their heads. Then they will be cleansed from their defilement. On the eighth day they must bring two turtledoves."

Samson believed the source of his strength was his unshorn locks, yet he shared the secret with Delilah. His actions appall modern readers because we saw how quick she was to betray him. Every time he shared his "secret", she tested him.

We marvel because Samson put the favors of a prostitute over obedience to God.

Yet God forgave him.

Samson's prayer at the end of his life was a penitent one,

where he referred to God as 'Ădônây Yᵉhôvâh.

'Ădônây, was the Lord's title used by the Jews instead of His name as a sign of reverence. 'Ădônây also means my Lord. Finally, Samson recognized God's true place in his life.

Samson also used God's covenant name Yᵉhôvâh. This name reveals who God is: the self-existent or eternal One. When Samson appealed to the Lord, He heard and answered him.

My friend, when we sin, the devil tells us God won't forgive us. Satan wants us to join him and his minions in hell. But God didn't create hell for us (Matthew 25:41), and He doesn't want us there. Salvation and forgiveness are available for those who believe and repent.

Seek forgiveness for your sins and be reconciled to your heavenly Father.

Prayer

Adonai Jehovah,

Have mercy on me, for I am a sinner. Forgive me for my sins and restore Your favor on me. Make me blameless in Your eyes. In Jesus' name, Amen.

Go Deeper

Read Judges 13–16

- What lessons does Samson's life teach you about sin?
- What do you learn about God's character?
- How can you safeguard yourself from following in Samson's

footsteps?

Key Points

1. Samson chose momentary pleasure and self-indulgence over communion with the Most High God.
2. Even after Samson's blatant disregard for God's requirements, the Lord forgave him.
3. God didn't create hell for us, but for the devil and his minions. Try not to end up there.

9

Forgiveness Might Require Restitution

*Psalm 86:5 NKJV — For You, Lord, are good, and ready to forgive,
And abundant in mercy to all those who call upon You.*

Manasseh stood in his throne room, one hand resting on his throne. He was home, and once again, king of Judah.

He was free—thanks to the Almighty Jehovah. He sank to his knees, tears of repentance and gratitude streaming down his face.

God had forgiven him after everything he'd done...

Manasseh became king of Judah after his father, Hezekiah, died. Hezekiah had been king for twenty-nine years. The people still talked about what a wonderful ruler his father had been.

They recounted the miracles God performed for Hezekiah. He heard the story so many times about how his father had been sick and about to die.

His father prayed, and the Lord sent the prophet Isaiah to tell him that God heard his prayer.

God made the sundial go back ten steps and gave Hezekiah an additional fifteen years to live. He was born during those years.

43

Was his father's notoriety why he'd chosen the opposite path? Had he meant to distinguish himself from his father by doing everything God said not to?

Shame twisted his guts as he remembered what he'd done. He rebuilt the high places his father had destroyed, built altars to the Baals and Asherah, and worshiped the hosts of heaven.

He built altars to idols in the court and temple of Jehovah. He sacrificed his sons to Baal, practiced sorcery, divination, and witchcraft, and consulted with mediums and psychics.

He incited the people of Judah to follow his evil ways, practicing idolatry until they were worse than the Amorites.

If that wasn't bad enough, he also murdered so many innocent people he could fill Jerusalem from one end to the other with their blood.

God sent His prophets to warn Manasseh and urged him to repent, but he didn't listen. Was it any wonder that God sent the commanders of the Assyrian armies and they took him prisoner?

They put a ring through his nose, bound him in bronze chains, and led him away to Babylon. He became a slave. A prisoner of war. They would have killed him, but God—

How could he have worshipped idols? None of them had the power to save. Baal and Asherah couldn't save him—only Jehovah.

When he realized the prophets were right—that God had judged him and Judah for what they'd done, he repented.

He cried out to the one true God, and the Lord heard him. The Lord restored his kingdom and returned him to Judah.

Manasseh rose to his feet, resolve strengthening. He would share his experiences with the people of Judah.

He would destroy the high places and purge the Temple of idols.

Judah would once again serve Jehovah if it was the last thing he accomplished before his death.

* * *

Sadly, the people of Judah continued to sacrifice at the high places. The Bible records they only sacrificed to the Lord (2 Chronicles 33:17), but that was not what God required.

> *Deuteronomy 12:1-6 NIV — These are the decrees and laws you must be careful to follow in the land that the LORD, the God of your ancestors, has given you to possess—as long as you live in the land.*
>
> *Destroy completely all the places on the high mountains, on the hills and under every spreading tree, where the nations you are dispossessing worship their gods.*
>
> *Break down their altars, smash their sacred stones and burn their Asherah poles in the fire; cut down the idols of their gods and wipe out their names from those places.*
>
> *You must not worship the Lord your God in their way.*
>
> *But you are to seek the place the Lord your God will choose from among all your tribes to put his Name there for his dwelling. To that place you must go;*
>
> *there bring your burnt offerings and sacrifices, your tithes and special gifts, what you have vowed to give and your freewill offerings, and the firstborn of your herds and flocks.*

God was specific about how and where He wanted to be worshipped. Their disobedience showed that their hearts had not truly returned to God.

Repentance does not always curtail the consequences of sin. Though Manasseh may have commanded his people to worship Jehovah, he couldn't change their hearts.

The Bible says Manasseh did more evil than the pagan nations God had driven out of the Promised Land. He slaughtered many innocent people. According to Jewish tradition, Manasseh killed the prophet Isaiah.

Yet God forgave Manasseh of his sins when he cried out with a repentant heart.

Manasseh made restitution after his return to Judah. He removed the idols, repaired the wall, and made thanksgiving and peace offerings to God.

My friend, if you need to make restorations after God has forgiven you, I encourage you to do so. Repay what you took, seek forgiveness from those you hurt. But understand that it's not always possible to return to the state prior to your transgressions.

The people you hurt may never forgive you. You may never fully repay them for what they lost. But never give up. From this day forth, live in a way that pleases God, understanding that some will never acknowledge how much you've changed.

Prayer

Father,

Thanks for forgiving me. Help me make restitution to those I hurt. Help me dedicate the rest of my life to You and to honor You with my actions and thoughts. In Jesus' name, Amen.

Go Deeper

Read 2 Kings 21:1-9, 2 Chronicles 33:1-20, Jeremiah 15:1-4

- What do these passages teach about the lingering effects of sin?
- What do you learn about God's capacity for forgiveness?
- What lessons can you implement in your life?

Key Points

1. God forgave Manasseh, one of the wickedest kings of Judah, when he repented and cried out to the Lord.
2. Forgiveness sometimes requires restitution. Repay and restore as much as possible.
3. God will forgive the vilest sinner if he repents.

10

God's Faithfulness Outweighs Your Sin

1 John 2:1 NIV — My dear children, I write this to you so that you will not sin. But if anybody does sin, we have an advocate with the Father—Jesus Christ, the Righteous One.

Gomer watched her husband. He was playing with their children, laughing as they ran back and forth across the lawn.

She didn't understand him. He was the strangest person she knew, and she didn't deserve him. After everything she had done, he remained faithful to her.

Shame nauseated her until she turned away from the domestic scene. She didn't belong here. But after everything Hosea had done for her...after she'd promised to be his wife...

Her life as Hosea's wife started years ago when he approached her father for her hand in marriage.

His request had shocked her, as she wasn't a virgin. In fact, Gomer's plethora of lovers had earned her a reputation as a promiscuous woman.

Men knew she was easy, so none of them came offering marriage.

They knew for the right price she'd sleep with them.

Her friends had stopped talking to her years ago. She didn't blame them. Reputations like hers tainted even the innocent.

Yet, Hosea insisted he would marry her because his God had told him to. She knew nothing about his God, but her father ordered her to marry the man.

He claimed it was a way to redeem her reputation, but she knew better. It was to remove the stain from his household. He would still be the man with the promiscuous daughter, but he wouldn't have to feed and clothe her anymore.

The first few years with Hosea, she tried. She kept his house, bore his children, entertained his few guests, but it wasn't enough. She wasn't enough.

How could she be?

At heart, she was the harlot everyone remembered while her husband was a pious man of God.

Hosea was always preaching about Jehovah and what He expected from His people, urging them to repent. He claimed God would destroy the Israelites for their unfaithfulness.

It was then she realized it: she was just like Israel.

Hosea was the ideal husband—loving, patient, a great provider, treating her as if she was precious. But he didn't know her secret.

She was damaged. Though her life was better than it had ever been, she lusted after other men.

It was like a call that thrummed in her blood, drowning out the beauty of her life and turning everything to ash. She resisted as long as she could until she just left.

Why should she continue to pretend that she deserved this virtuous man?

She found a disreputable man who took her in. He didn't care that she was another man's wife, or the mother of three children.

Sometimes, she thought he considered it was a badge of honor—something he could boast about. He had taken her from her husband and family.

Gomer knew she'd made the wrong choice, but what was she supposed to do? It's not as if she could go back to Hosea. No, her husband had suffered enough embarrassment because of her.

She plastered on a smile and picked up the platter to bring to her new man, her jailer. She almost spilled the entire contents when she spotted his guest.

Hosea.

What was her husband doing here?

"Gomer," Ray beckoned her over, a glint in his eyes. "Look who came for a visit."

She crept to Ray's side, keeping one eye on him and the other on Hosea. The greed in Ray's eyes did not bode well for whatever came next.

"Sit here." Ray patted his knee.

Everything in Gomer rebelled, but if she didn't obey, there would be a price. She had the wounds to prove it.

She slid the tray onto the low table between the two men and slunk to Ray. Hopefully, he'd think she was being sultry, not resisting him. But had she known who he was entertaining, she'd have risked his ire rather than face her husband under these circumstances.

She perched on Ray's knee, pretending she was sitting on a regular chair. But he was having none of that. He hauled her against him, his intimate handling of her body leaving no doubt of their relationship.

"Hosea tells me you two have a history."

She smothered a groan at Ray's gloating voice. Why had Hosea come? She averted her eyes, not wanting to see the disgust and loathing in his.

Was this his way of paying her back for what she'd done to their family?

"Your husband," Ray said the words like a slur, "wants you back."

"What?" Her chin jutted up to meet Hosea's gaze. She must have misheard.

"Yes, my dear," Ray stroked her arm, his touch sending shivers of disgust down her spine. "He has paid handsomely for you." He shoved her out of his lap.

She spilled on the floor, her arms barely flying out in time to prevent her face from slamming into the ground.

Pain shot through her, radiating from where her hip and elbow had connected with the floor.

Ray stood, a sneer marring his features. "Be gone when I return. Take nothing except the clothes you're wearing." He stepped over her, leaving her behind like trash.

"Are you hurt?" Hosea bent, running gentle fingers over her limbs as he checked for injuries.

How could he be so kind when all she'd brought him was shame?

"Hosea—" Tears and shame clogged her throat and she couldn't speak.

"Shh." He pressed a finger against her lips. "Don't speak." He helped her stand, allowing her to lean against him.

"You'll live with me for the rest of your life. But please, stop your prostitution. You won't have sex with anyone, and that includes me."

She gaped at him. Had he truly said what she thought he had?

* * *

God instructed the prophet Hosea to marry a promiscuous woman. This was an allegory for God's relationship with Israel.

The Lord did everything for Israel. He rescued them from

slavery in Egypt and brought them into the Promise Land. He provided them with bountiful harvests, gave them houses, blessed their wombs...

But rather than worship the Creator, they turned to idols. God sent prophets to warn His people, but they would not listen.

As you read the book of Hosea, you will see God warning His people repeatedly that if they did not turn back to Him, if they did not repent, He would destroy them.

There was also a thread of hope. God spoke of a future when they would be faithful, when He would once again call them His children, and be their God.

Hosea is a sad account of the unfaithfulness of God's people, but it is also a poignant reminder of His faithfulness.

The chatter of our world distracts us from worshiping God. It's easy to get caught up in various activities or to spend hours on the internet.

Yet we find it difficult to spend a few minutes with God. We fall asleep in church or rush through our devotional time.

My friend, if this you, it's not a judgment of your behavior. It's an encouragement to turn back to God.

Our heavenly Father is waiting with open arms for you to return to Him. Seek His forgiveness and accept the love He so willingly bestows on you.

Prayer

Abba,

Please forgive me for my sins. You are a loving Father and I'm grateful for the grace that flows from You. Help me remain faithful as You are faithful. In Jesus' name, Amen.

Go Deeper

Read Hosea

- Can you identify the ways the Israelites hurt God?
- What lessons do you learn about God's faithfulness?
- What parallels do you see between the Israelites and your-self?
- How might you learn from the story of Hosea and Gomer?

Key Points

1. The story of Hosea and Gomer is an allegorical depiction of God's relationship with the Israelites.
2. Though the Israelites' unfaithfulness incited God's wrath, He offered a message of hope if they would return to Him.
3. No matter what you've done, God is waiting with open arms to forgive you.

11

God's Mercy Is Not Limitless

Isaiah 55:7 NKJV — Let the wicked forsake his way, And the unrighteous man his thoughts; Let him return to the LORD, And He will have mercy on him; And to our God, For He will abundantly pardon.

I stared at the vast kingdom before me. Babylon was a beautiful place indeed. There was a time when I mistakenly thought I was the one who had built this immense kingdom.

I shook my head at my folly.

Eight years ago, I had a disturbing dream. I saw an enormous tree that became strong until its top reached heaven, and it was visible to the entire earth.

It was a beautiful tree, with abundant fruit where the beasts of the field gathered beneath it and the birds lived in its branches. The tree was so bountiful it fed everything.

One day, a messenger from heaven came down and made an announcement. He said, "Chop down the tree. Sever its branches. Strip off its leaves and scatter its fruit. Let the beasts run from under it and the birds scatter from its branches.

"But leave the stump of its root in the earth. It will be bound with a band of iron and bronze and remain among the tender grass of the field. Let the dew of heaven wet him. Let his portion be with the beasts of the Earth.

"Change his mind from that of a man and give him a beast's mind. And let seven years pass over him. This is the decision of the Holy One so that everyone may know that the Most High rules over the kingdoms of the earth.

"It is God who raises kings. He gives kingdoms to anyone He chooses, even the lowliest of people."

None of my wise men, advisors, or astrologers could figure out what the dream meant, except Daniel. The Jewish man was wiser than all my advisors. He had a connection to the gods, and they spoke to him.

When Daniel heard my dream, he was distressed. He refused to tell me what it meant until I assured him he would come to no harm. He explained I was the tree and his God had plans to cut me down.

Daniel urged me to repent of my evil ways. He told me I needed to acknowledge his God as Supreme over the Earth. If I didn't, I would become like an animal for seven years.

I didn't believe him, of course. Whoever heard of a man acting like an animal? For twelve months, I continued as if nothing had happened. I was walking on the roof of my palace when a surge of pride overcame me.

"Look at this great Babylon that I have built by my power," I boasted. "It is a royal sign of the glory of my majesty." Before I was done speaking, a voice came from heaven and said, "Oh, King Nebuchadnezzar, this message is for you. You are no longer the ruler of this kingdom. You will be driven from human society and live in the fields like a wild animal and eat grass like a cow.

"Seven years will pass while you live this way until you learn that

the Most High rules over the world's kingdoms and give them to anyone He chooses."

For 7 years, I lived like an animal. No, I was an animal, living outdoors under the elements, in heat and cold. I couldn't speak. I became an oddity. A marvel.

Everyone believed I had offended the gods. But there is only one God. The Hebrew God is the Most High.

When I acknowledged Jehovah was God, He restored everything to me. I became a man again. I was no longer an animal—no longer a beast.

As Daniel had said, God restored my kingdom. My advisors sought me out. Everything was as it was before I went mad. Except for one thing. I now acknowledge that there is a God in heaven and He only will I serve.

* * *

King Nebuchadnezzar was a powerful Babylonian King who tested God on multiple occasions. The first account we have that God had a message for Nebuchadnezzar is in Daniel 2.

Nebuchadnezzar dreamed of a statue. He saw a stone, carved out of nothing that hurled against the giant statue and destroyed it. Nebuchadnezzar understood his dream was important, but he couldn't figure out what it meant.

Nebuchadnezzar was determined to understand his disturbing dream, but didn't trust his magicians and astrologers to tell him the truth. Instead, he made it a test.

If his magicians and astrologists told him the dream, then he could be certain they understood its meaning. Of course, this was an impossible task. No one can determine what a person dreams unless he's first told.

But there is a God in heaven who knows dreams. God gives dreams and visions to people.

Daniel expressed that King Nebuchadnezzar was the head of gold. He told the king another less powerful kingdom would come after him. Babylon would not remain the dominant world power forever. There would be other kingdoms, and each would be less powerful than the last.

Rather than praise the God of heaven for revealing this truth to him, Nebuchadnezzar used his dream as a blueprint to build an idol. He compelled everyone in his kingdom to bow and worship the statue.

When Shadrach, Meshach and Abednego heard the special song that signified the call to worship, they did not bow. But some astrologers went and informed the king. Nebuchadnezzar became enraged when he learned of their disobedience.

He was determined to destroy them, and commanded them to worship the idol. If they did not, he would put them in the fiery furnace. The three Hebrew men refused, and Nebuchadnezzar had his second experience with the Most High God.

The fire instantly killed the men who threw the three Hebrews into the furnace. Yet, Shadrach Meshach and Abednego were unharmed. Not only that, there was a fourth man in the fire.

According to Nebuchadnezzar, the fourth man resembled a god (Daniel 3:25). This was Jesus Himself, walking among the flames with His faithful servants.

Nebuchadnezzar acknowledged that the God of Shadrach Meshach and Abednego was powerful. He made a decree that no one in his kingdom should say a word against the God of the Hebrews or they would be torn limb from limb and their houses destroyed.

But an indeterminate time later, he forgot the lesson. Despite

Daniel's warning, he thought he had built Babylon, not Jehovah.

Nebuchadnezzar's experience teaches us two major things about God's forgiveness:

1. God is gracious and merciful toward us. He did not destroy Nebuchadnezzar after he built the idol. He didn't destroy him after the king forced everyone into idolatry.

Even after God gave him the second dream, He didn't destroy Nebuchadnezzar then. But God's grace has a limit. There will come a time when everyone must account for their actions and their deeds.

2. God's grace, forgiveness, and mercy will always be greater than our sins. For seven years, Nebuchadnezzar became like a field animal. He wasn't conscious of anything except his base instincts.

God could have killed him, but He didn't. He kept him alive so Nebuchadnezzar would know that Jehovah was God.

My friend, are you living as if God doesn't exist? If you are, this is your wake-up call to remember that God is merciful, but His mercy has a limit. I don't say this to scare you. This is to encourage you to do what is right. It's a reminder that when we humble ourselves and repent of our sins, God forgives us every time.

Prayer

Dear heavenly Father,

I don't always do what is right. Sometimes I remain in my disobedience and sin after countless warnings. But I'm thankful for Your mercy and grace, and that You don't treat me as my sin deserves.

Help me to never forget who You are, Almighty God—the one who created heaven and earth, the seas, and everything in them. Help me live blameless before You. In Jesus' name, Amen.

Go Deeper

Read Daniel 2-4

- What does the account of King Nebuchadnezzar and Jehovah teach you about God?
- Have you had similar experiences where God reached out, asking you to repent of sin, but you remained unrelenting? How did that story end? What did it teach you about God?
- Do you believe God had sufficient reasons to punish Nebuchadnezzar? Why or why not?

Key Points

1. Everything we have comes from God and we should praise Him for what He's done.
2. God is merciful, but eventually, everyone has to account for their actions.
3. Heed God's warnings before it's too late.

12

Show Mercy As You've Received Mercy

Mark 11:26 KJV — But if ye do not forgive, neither will your Father which is in heaven forgive your trespasses.

Moshe gripped the bars of his cell, squeezing the metal beneath his palm. This was his fault. He hadn't understood the nuances of grace.

"If only I could get a do-over."

John, his new cell mate padded over to him. The young man's clothes were raggedy, but then, so were his and everyone else's.

"What would you do differently?" John's expression was curious, and Moshe had a strong urge to pass on the lesson to the younger man.

If—when John—made it out of here, maybe the lesson would serve him so he didn't make the same mistake Moshe had.

He met John's gaze. "I used to work for a wealthy man." He named his former employer, and John's eyes widened.

His response didn't surprise Moshe; his ex-boss was famous.

"I had some difficulties and took a few payroll loans." His wife had gotten sick, then one of his daughters. His basement had flooded, *and the damage had been costly to repair.*

He didn't go into the details, as that wasn't the point of his tale.

"At first, I had a small debt. But as time went by, I borrowed more money until it became greater than I could repay in one lifetime."

In retrospect, he could have avoided many of the later loans. But he'd began living beyond his means, depending on the loans his employer willingly extended.

John winced. "What happened?" He scanned the cramped room that was not big enough for one person. "Is that why you're here?"

"Yes, and no."

It wasn't uncommon for people to be sent to debtor's jail to work off the debts they'd incurred.

"I don't understand."

Moshe clapped the man on his shoulder. "Let's work as I explain." He shuffled to the narrow cot and bent to straighten the thin sheets.

Their jailer would be there in a few minutes and he insisted they spread their beds, or he withheld a meal.

"One day, my employer had his accountant go through his books. He arranged meetings with those who owed him. I was first on that list because I had the largest debt."

"Is that when he threw you in jail?"

"Not quite. That was his initial plan, but when I thought about leaving my wife and children without protection, I fell at his feet and begged for mercy."

John's lips pressed together in displeasure. "He said 'No' , didn't he? Men like him enjoy lauding their power over the rest of us."

"Actually," Moshe smoothed a palm over the sheet. "He said 'Yes', and wiped my slate clean."

"You're joking." John's eyes rounded with surprise. "So what happened?"

Moshe swallowed hard. He needed courage to tell the rest of his tale.

"I bumped into someone who owed me a few dollars."

John grinned. "I bet you were so happy after having your debt forgiven that you did the same for him."

Moshe winced. If only. "The opposite. I insisted that the man paid me what he owed. When he begged for mercy, I ignored him." Moshe's shoulders bunched around his ears. He wasn't proud of what he'd done.

"I had him sent to debtor's prison."

John gaped. "How could you?"

"I was stupid and greedy." Mean-spirited. Petty. He had a never-ending list of derogatory names for himself. "My coworkers weren't happy. Many of them knew what the boss had done for me. They told him how I'd treated my colleague, and the rest, as they say, is history."

Moshe lifted his shoulder. "My boss rescinded his cancellation of my debts and put me in jail until I pay it off. I'll be here for the rest of my life."

* * *

The parable of the unmerciful servant in Matthew 18:21-35 was Jesus' response to Peter's question:

"Lord, how many times shall I forgive my brother or sister who sins against me? Up to seven times?" (Matthew 18:21)

It was an illustration that those who receive forgiveness should show grace to others.

Who can say they don't require grace? Romans 3:23 tells us we've all sinned and come short of the glory of God.

Since God lavishly bestows grace on us, shouldn't we do the same for others?

Sadly, we don't always see how our actions reflect our heavenly Father. Too often, we don't treat each other the way we would want to be treated.

My friend, this principle is so important to God that Jesus repeated it several times during His earthly ministry.

Matthew 6:12 KJV — And forgive us our debts, as we forgive our debtors.

Matthew 6:14-15 KJV — For if ye forgive men their trespasses, your heavenly Father will also forgive you:
But if ye forgive not men their trespasses, neither will your Father forgive your trespasses.

Matthew 7:1-2 KJV — Judge not, that ye be not judged.
For with what judgment ye judge, ye shall be judged: and with what measure ye mete, it shall be measured to you again.

Luke 6:37 KJV — Judge not, and ye shall not be judged: condemn not, and ye shall not be condemned: forgive, and ye shall be forgiven:

Forgiveness is important to God, and He wants us to forgive others in kind.

Prayer

Dear Lord,
Forgive me for my sins and help me forgive those who hurt me. I want to be more like You. Have mercy on me, O Lord, and

teach me to show mercy. In Jesus' name, Amen.

Go Deeper

Read Matthew 18:21-35

- Why do you think Peter asked Jesus how often he should forgive others?
- How do Peter's and the unmerciful servant's attitude toward forgiveness sometimes mimic our own?
- What if God had a limit for the number of times He'd forgave us? What would life be like?

Key Points

1. The unmerciful servant received grace from his employer, but he didn't pass it on to his fellow man.
2. We should forgive others because God forgives us.
3. Offering mercy to someone is an opportunity to show what God has done for you.

13

Jesus Teaches You How to Show Mercy

Romans 8:13 NIV — For if you live according to the flesh, you will die; but if by the Spirit you put to death the misdeeds of the body, you will live.

Anaya clutched the sheet against her naked body as the men dragged her along the streets. Their presence attracted attention as more and more people joined the throng.

One second she had been in the middle of a clandestine meeting and the next, the door had burst open and a group of men rushed in, hauling her out of bed. She barely had time to grab a sheet to cover herself.

Not that it mattered. She knew how this story ended. They would take her into the square, where the townspeople would stone her to death.

Shame hung heavy on her shoulders, making it difficult to raise her head. Not that she wanted to. The jeers from the growing throng reminded her of what she'd done wrong.

Rough hands dragged her through a narrow door. Her nose twitched as the scent of the burned flesh filled her lungs.

Wait.

Her head snapped up. This was not the town square. They'd brought her into the temple where the famous rabbi stood in front of the crowds, teaching.

She backed away, limbs shaking. Why had they brought her here?

One of her accusers grabbed her upper arm, his grip punishing. "Where do you think you're going?" he snarled, his foul breath hot against her ear. "We're making an example of you today."

He hauled her before the group. "Teacher, we caught this woman in the act of adultery. The Law of Moses commands us to stone such women. What do you say?"

Panic fluttered in her chest. That wasn't what the Law said—both the adulterer and the adulteress should die.

Anaya's gaze frantically scanned the gathering. Where was Elias? Had they taken him some place else? Had they already killed him?

Her heart thudded in her ears, making it difficult for her to hear.

There. Out of the corner of her eye, she spotted her lover—clothed in the middle of the mob.

How?

Her lips trembled as she struggled to make sense of what she was seeing.

It had been a setup.

Her shoulders slumped at the realization. Her lover had conspired with the scribes and Pharisees to disgrace her.

She refocused on the rabbi, holding her breath for this man to condemn her according to their Law, but he said nothing.

He stooped, writing with his fingers in the dust. Had he heard them?

How could he not? The more he ignored them, the more frantic their questions became, the louder they shouted.

After an eternity, the rabbi straightened and faced the rabble.

"Let the person who is without sin throw the first stone at her."
Then he stooped again and wrote on the ground.

She squeezed her eyes shut, bracing for the blow.

Oh, why hadn't she obeyed the Law? If she had, she wouldn't be
in this pickle.

Oh, God, please. Have mercy on me. It was wrong to have an
intimate relationship with a married man. I won't do it again.
Please.

Did God listen to sinners? Would He hear her cry? Would He
answer? The teachers of the Law had condemned her. What hope
did she have?

The group mumbled among themselves, their dissatisfaction
evident.

This was it. Someone would throw a stone at her.

"Hmph! This is ridiculous!"

A man bumped into her and her eyes flew open as she stumbled
forward. Another pushed past her, his expression harsh, and then
another. They were leaving!

Her mouth dropped open as they filed out, one at a time. First the
older ones and then the youngest until she was alone with the rabbi
and the people in the temple.

But she wasn't safe yet. This man could turn on her at any moment
and start a new mob.

He stood and stared into her eyes, his expression gentle. Had she
ever seen so much love in someone's gaze?

"Woman, where are your accusers?" His voice was kind. "Has no
man condemned you?"

She cleared her throat, glancing behind her to ensure the mob had
truly gone.

"No man, sir."

The rabbi smiled at her. "Neither do I condemn you. Go, and sin *no more."*

Anaya tightened the wrap around her bodice. This was what she'd prayed for—a second chance.

Tears streamed down her cheeks as the miracle she'd experienced settled into her spirit.

She should be dead, but had received another chance to obey the commandments and serve the God of her forefathers.

She turned and walked away, the rabbi's voice ringing in her ears.

"I am the light of the world. He that follows me shall not walk in darkness, but shall have the light of life."

* * *

Moses' Law about the treatment of adulterers was clear.

> *Deuteronomy 22:22 KJV — If a man be found lying with a woman married to an husband, then they shall both of them die, both the man that lay with the woman, and the woman: so shalt thou put away evil from Israel.*

The scribes and Pharisees claimed they caught the woman in the adulterous act, yet they brought her alone to stand trial for her crime (John 8:4).

They offered mercy to the man, but there was no grace for the woman. The Bible doesn't tell us where her partner was during the accusation, but it doesn't matter.

Jesus' response is what we need to focus on.

The Israelites, especially the scribes and Pharisees, were fanatical about keeping the Law, at least, as they interpreted it.

There was no room for grace. If you messed up, you paid the penalty.

Romans 3:23 tells us that all have sinned and come short of God's standards. But I'm glad it didn't end there.

> *Romans 3:23-24 NLT — For everyone has sinned; we all fall short of God's glorious standard.*
> *Yet God, with undeserved kindness, declares that we are righteous. He did this through Christ Jesus when he freed us from the penalty for our sins.*

Jesus' blood cleanses us from sin and washes away our unrighteousness. Oh, praise the Lord that we can go into His throne room and receive mercy and grace.

My friend, I don't know what sins you struggled with—what you may still wrestle with. But there is hope in Christ.

Jesus forgives our sins. All you have to do is ask and receive a pardon from the Prince of Peace.

Prayer

Dear Lord,

Thanks for sending Your Son to die for my sins. Please cover me in His righteousness. In Jesus' name, Amen.

Go Deeper

Read John 8:1-11

- Why do you think the scribes and Pharisees only brought the woman to Jesus?

- Has someone ever accused you of something? How did you feel during the accusation?
- Why do you believe Jesus responded as He did?
- What lessons from this account can you apply to your life?

Key Points

1. According to the Law of Moses, the adulterer and adulteress should be stoned to death. Yet the scribes and Pharisees only brought the woman to Jesus for punishment.
2. Jesus taught that mercy is an integral part of serving God.
3. When God forgives you, do not return to your sin.

14

Grace and Love Are Intertwined

Isaiah 1:18 NKJV — "Come now, and let us reason together," Says the LORD, "Though your sins are like scarlet, They shall be as white as snow; Though they are red like crimson, They shall be as wool."

"Did you hear?" Puah whispered excitedly as she knelt beside Ahava. "The rabbi's having dinner at Simon's house."

Ahava's heartbeat escalated. Jesus was here...in her community, where she could visit Him.

"Which Simon is He dining with?" She kept her tone casual while she continued kneading the dough.

Puah pursed her lips. "Who do you think?"

Ahava's heart sank. Simon the Pharisee would never let her near his house. The man knew her sinful past and never let her forget it.

Whenever they met in public, he crossed to the other side of the street and looked down his nose at her, as if he believed she could contaminate him by contact.

"The rabbi's coming with His disciples. Can you imagine the crowds? I plan to stand outside Simon's house so I can glimpse the

71

great teacher."

A glimmer of an idea occurred to her. Maybe if she...

Puah continued to chatter while Ahava made a plan.

Later that evening, Ahava pulled her shawl to better cover her face as she pressed through the crowd. As Puah had said, the entire community and some from nearby towns gathered outside the Pharisee's house.

She clutched the alabaster jar with its precious contents closer to her chest as she wove through the throng. Jesus was inside that house and she would get to Him.

When she finally made it through the crowd, her emotions overwhelmed her. This Man had saved her and given her a shot at a new life.

Tears streamed from her eyes until she was sobbing. Weeping.

Ahava knelt at the rabbi's feet. She had been so lost until she met this Man who showed her the way to God.

Tears plopped onto His feet, and she leaned forward to wipe them away with her hair. She kissed His feet and lovingly anointed them with the perfume from her jar. Her ministrations attracted Simon's attention, but she didn't care.

The Pharisee stood over her, mouth curled in his usual sneer. "If this man was a prophet, he would know what kind of woman is touching him—that she is a sinner."

Jesus turned. "Simon, I have something to say to you."

Ahava watched the interaction through her curtain of hair.

Simon's lips curved into a fake smile. "Tell me, Master."

"There was a certain creditor who had two debtors. One owed five hundred dollars, and the other fifty. When they couldn't pay, he forgave them both. Which of them will love him more?"

Simon stroked his chin. "The one who had the bigger debt."

Jesus nodded. "You are correct."

Then Jesus turned toward her and said to Simon, "Do you see this woman? I came into your house and you didn't give me any water for my feet, but she wet my feet with her tears and wiped them with her hair.

"You didn't greet me with a kiss, but this woman, from the time I entered, has not stopped kissing my feet.

"You didn't anoint my head with oil, but she has poured perfume on my feet. Therefore, I tell you, her many sins have been forgiven—as her great love has shown. But the one who has been forgiven little loves little."

Then Jesus said to Ahava, "Your sins are forgiven."

* * *

In Jesus' time, it was customary to provide guests with water to wash the dust from their feet before they entered your home.

In wealthy households, a servant would wash the guest's feet.

The host would greet the visitor with a kiss and anoint his head with oil as a sign of respect.

Though Simon invited Jesus to dine with him, he ignored the common niceties. While we don't know Simon's reason, we can theorize that, as a Pharisee, he considered himself Jesus' superior.

Bible scholars believe Simon didn't want to anger his peers by treating Jesus with the customary respect offered to a rabbi.

But that's not the point of this lesson. Jesus pointed out that the person who has a greater debt forgiven would have more reasons to love.

Perhaps you've experienced this truth in your life. The person who God rescued from a life of sin—things like prostitution, addiction, or abuse—are more vocal about their faith.

Maybe you've experienced God's grace, and it makes you more passionate about Him. You can't understand why everyone doesn't give their lives to God and serve Him.

My friend, forgiveness changes us. It wraps around our hearts and transforms us from the inside out.

This quote attributed to Martin Luther encapsulates God's forgiveness:

"When I look at myself, I don't see how I can be saved. But when I look at Christ, I don't see how I can be lost."

The Pharisees of Jesus' time, believed keeping the Law perfectly, would save them. This often meant they were more concerned with the rules than true submission to God.

They performed the actions but had none of the heart.

Jesus came to show us God's heart. Yes, God wants obedience, but He's more concerned with the condition of our hearts.

Prayer

Dear Lord,

I cannot save myself. I'm grateful for Jesus' sacrifice that restores my good standing with You. May I never forget it's because of Your grace that I'm still alive. In Jesus' name, Amen.

Go Deeper

Read Luke 7:36-50

- What kind of lifestyle do you think God saved the woman from?

- Do you have anything in common with her? What has God rescued you from?
- If you were in that woman's position, what would you be praising God for?

Key Points

1. Simon invited Jesus to his house but didn't offer Him the common courtesies of the time.
2. The woman anointed Jesus with her tears and precious perfume as an act of love.
3. The more you have been forgiven, the more you'll love God.

15

Your Heavenly Father Is Waiting to Forgive

Micah 7:18 NKJV — Who is a God like You, Pardoning iniquity And passing over the transgression of the remnant of His heritage? He does not retain His anger forever, Because He delights in mercy.

Hallel smiled at his younger son, Ronen. Of his two children, Ronen was the more impulsive.

His boy was prone to flights of imagination that sometimes worried Hallel, but he prayed God would teach his son temperance.

Ronen paced the large office, a sure sign that he had something to say. Hallel steepled his fingers and waited.

"Father, I want my share of the estate."

Hallel's eyebrow shot up. "Pardon me?"

Ronen stopped pacing and met his gaze. "I want to be independent and explore the world. This life," Ronen spread his hands, "is not for me."

Hallel pursed his lips as he considered what Ronen asked. There were so many things wrong with the boy's request, but he knew *from experience that arguing with Ronen was futile.*

The boy wouldn't learn without the hard knocks of experience.

"Very well."

Hallel met with his accountant and divided his estate. He deposited Ronen's share into his account. The next morning, the boy was gone.

His initial reports were full of excitement as Ronen visited various countries, partook in local festivities and made new friends. Soon, the reports stopped.

Hallel took to pacing the long driveway, hoping for news of his son. One day as he peered into the distance, he spotted a figure limping up the winding path.

"Could that be...?" He squinted, holding a hand above his eyes to shield them from the bright sun.

The figure was thin, his hair disheveled and his clothing tattered, but...

He gasped. It was Ronen. His son had come home!

Hallel ran down the driveway, stumbling over his unsteady feet. "My son!"

He opened his arms, embraced his long-lost son, and kissed his cheeks.

"Father," Ronen's voice was husky with unshed tears. "I've sinned against heaven and against you. I'm no longer worthy of being called your son."

Hallel drew Ronen into the house. It didn't matter that dust and grime covered him or that he stunk as if he hadn't bathed for a week...his son was alive.

"Quick!" He called to the maid. "Bring the best robe for Ronen. Put a ring on his finger and shoes on his feet."

"Linus," he called to the cook. "Prepare your best dishes. We're having a feast to celebrate. For my son was dead and is alive again.

He was lost and is found."

In the middle of the celebration, a servant attracted his attention.

"Sir," the young man leaned closer to be heard over the loud, pulsing music. "Yonah is outside. He wants to speak with you."

Hallel frowned. "Why doesn't Yonah join us inside? We're celebrating his brother's return."

The servant lowered his gaze. "He refuses to come in."

With a sigh, Hallel left his guests and went outside to his older son.

The damp night air pickled his skin, and Hallel once again praised God for bringing his son home.

Yonah paced the length of the backyard, his movements agitated and angry.

"Yonah?" Concern made Hallel's heart beat faster. "Why aren't you at the party? Is everything alright?"

"No!" Yonah whirled, a sneer contorting his features. "Nothing is alright! For years, I've slaved for you and never disobeyed your orders. Yet you never gave me even a kid so I could celebrate with my friends.

"But when the son who squandered your property with prostitutes comes home, you kill the fattened calf for him!"

"Yonah," Hallel implored, "you are always with me, and everything I have is yours.

"Shouldn't we celebrate and rejoice because of your brother's return? Ronen was dead and is alive again. He was lost and is found. Why aren't you happy he's home?"

* * *

In ancient Israel, the only way for a son to inherit was after his father's death. When the prodigal son went to his father for his inheritance, he was telling his parent that he wished he were dead.

He was tired of waiting for what he believed belonged to him.

When the son left home, he had no thought about the future. He was only living for that day. But the mismanagement of funds and his profligate lifestyle soon squandered what it had taken years for his father to acquire.

The prodigal son was at his lowest—low enough to consider eating pig food.

The Bible tells us he came to his senses. The prodigal son recognized he had dishonored his father. He understood that a servant in his father's household received better treatment than he did.

When the prodigal son decided to return home, it was an acceptance that he had treated his father poorly. It required him to humble himself.

Like the prodigal son, you and I have sinned against our heavenly Father. We took God's gifts and wasted them in the devil's kingdom.

But here's the beautiful thing. God is waiting for us to come to our senses.

He wants us to return home. He is ready to kill the fatted calf and celebrate our return.

Are you too proud to ask for forgiveness and humble yourself before God?

My friend, if you have unconfessed sin, waste no more time chastising yourself. Take a moment to humbly go before your heavenly Father in prayer. He's waiting with open arms to welcome you home.

Prayer

Dear Lord,

I have sinned and I'm not worthy to be called Your daughter. Please forgive me for everything I've done that brought shame and dishonor to You.

Receive me into Your presence again, in Jesus' name, Amen.

Go Deeper

Read Luke 15:11–32.

- What do you think prompted the prodigal son to ask for his share of his father's estate?
- How does his actions parallel our treatment of our heavenly Father?
- What does the attitude of the older son teach you about unforgiveness?
- How do you see parallels of both sons' attitudes in your life?

Key Points

1. By asking for his portion of the estate, the prodigal son was telling his father that he couldn't wait until his death to inherit.
2. The older son displayed a lack of understanding for his father's mercy. Be careful not to imitate him.

3. Your heavenly Father is always watching for your return, waiting to welcome you with open arms.

16

If You Deny Jesus, He'll Deny You

Hebrews 4:16 NKJV — Let us therefore come boldly to the throne of grace, that we may obtain mercy and find grace to help in time of need.

Peter reclined at the table with John and his colleagues. It was the Passover, and Jesus had introduced them to a new ritual. He wouldn't admit it aloud, but Peter struggled to understand some of Jesus' teachings.

"Simon, Simon."

Peter sat up as Jesus called his name. "Yes, Lord?"

"Satan demanded to have you that he might sift you like wheat."

Peter's heart lurched. What?

"But I have prayed for you that your faith doesn't fail," Jesus continued. "And when you have turned again, strengthen your brothers."

What was Jesus talking about? He would never turn away from his Lord and would follow Him anywhere.

"Lord, I am ready to go to prison and die with You."

Jesus gazed at him, eyes soft with compassion. "Peter, before the rooster crows twice today, you'll deny Me three times."

He was pondering Jesus' strange words when the most dramatic day of his life unfolded.

Judas, one of their friends, showed up with soldiers and the leaders, and captured Jesus. Peter was afraid they would seize him, too, so he ran. All of the disciples did—just as Jesus had predicted hours earlier.

He and John followed the throng to the high priest's house.

It was cold, and the servants and officials stood around a fire to keep warm. Peter stood with them, warming himself.

One of the servant girls looked at him. "You were with Jesus, weren't you?"

He avoided her eyes. "I was not."

The high priest questioned Jesus about His disciples and teachings while Peter held his breath. Jesus had warned about this, but how could they take Him?

He had done nothing wrong. He was the Messiah, wasn't He?

About an hour passed, and another servant girl narrowed her eyes at him. "You were with Jesus."

"No, I was not." He swore an oath. "I do not know what you are talking about."

The trial continued, but it was a sham. The elders and leaders were punishing Jesus for not supporting their teachings.

Peter's heart hurt for his teacher's pain and embarrassment.

How could they disgrace the rabbi like that? How could they put on the farce of a trial right before the Passover?

A relative of the high priest's servant pointed at Peter. "You were with that Man. Your language betrays you. Besides," the man smirked, "you are Galilean, just like Him."

Sweat rolled down his back. Would they arrest him, too? Would they subject him to a farce of a trial? Would he die tonight because *of his affiliation with Jesus?*

"I do not know this Man." Peter swore in a way he hadn't in years.

At that moment, the rooster crowed. Jesus turned to look at Peter and he remembered his Lord's words. Peter went outside and wept bitterly.

* * *

If this had been the end of Peter's story, it would have been a mournful tale. But Peter, encouraged by Jesus' charge in John 21:1-19, became a mighty leader in the early church.

As Jesus commanded, he strengthened the brethren and was a great source of inspiration and motivation.

Jesus told His disciples:

> *Matthew 10:32-33 NLT — "Everyone who acknowledges me publicly here on earth, I will also acknowledge before my Father in heaven.*
>
> *"But everyone who denies me here on earth, I will also deny before my Father in heaven."*

Maybe you haven't been the stalwart defender of your faith that you should be. Perhaps you had the chance to share your faith and didn't. Or you're not as passionate about evangelism as others...

The enemy would like nothing more than for you to drift away from God. He wants you to believe your sins are unforgivable. But don't lose hope.

You can decide today that will change the trajectory of your life.

Like Peter, you can allow the Holy Spirit to transform one of the lowest moments of your life into a testimony.

Prayer

Father, I'm not always a great ambassador for You. Sometimes my actions reflect my flesh rather than the Spirit living within me.

Help me be more like You. When I make a mistake, help me get up and press forward, in Jesus' name, Amen.

Go Deeper

Read Matthew 26:31-35, 47-75; Mark 14:27-31, 66-72; Luke 22:31-34, 54-62; John 13:31-38, 18:15-26, 21:1-19

- How do you think Peter felt when Jesus predicted his betrayal and afterward?
- Have you ever denied Christ?
- What can you do to safeguard your faith so you'll always boldly declare your belief in God?

Key Points

1. Jesus predicted Peter's denial of Him at the trial. But Jesus also foretold Peter's stalwart defense of the faith.
2. Pressure can create an environment where denying your

affiliation with Christ feels right.

3. If you falter in your faith, repent and keep pressing forward. You may become a powerful influence on other believers.

17

Forgiveness Can Elevate Your Position

Ephesians 4:32 KJV — And be ye kind one to another, tenderhearted, forgiving one another, even as God for Christ's sake hath forgiven you.

A messenger arrived in Philemon's household. This wasn't just any messenger, he came from the apostle Paul who was a prisoner because he believed in Jesus.

Philemon hurried to greet the man. It didn't matter that he had business to take care of. This was more important.

He accepted the papyrus from the messenger and ordered his servants to provide refreshments and a bowl of water to wash the man's feet.

Philemon eagerly uncurled the scroll, anticipating a word of encouragement from his mentor.

His lips curved as he read the scroll. How wonderful that the man of God recognized what he'd done for the church.

It had come at great personal and financial sacrifice, but it was worth it. The news about Jesus needed to be shared and he was glad to do his part.

A frown marred his brow as he read Paul's comment. He'd do anything for the apostle. Without Paul, he wouldn't have learned the good news about his Savior.

Why did Paul believe he had to coax him into doing anything?

The hand holding the letter trembled as he read further.

No.

Paul couldn't possibly expect him to accept Onesimus, that slave who'd betrayed his trust, stolen from him, and run away. Expect Philemon to treat him not as a slave but as a brother? To treat Onesimus, that traitor, like Paul's son?

How could Paul ask this of him? It was too much.

His conscience niggled at him. Hadn't he pledged to do whatever the apostle asked? But no. He tossed the scroll aside and paced the room.

Paul was a Roman citizen. He knew the law. He understood that Philemon could do whatever he chose to Onesimus. The slave was his property, and Philemon had the right to demand restitution by imprisonment or other punishment.

Paul acted as if he was doing Philemon a favor by sending Onesimus to him. It was the right thing to do. The law.

But what of the Law of God? What of his promise to treat others with the same favor God had shown him?

What of his desire to be a light shining in a dark world as Christ had commanded His followers?

Philemon stooped to pick up the scroll. He skipped the greeting and went to the crux of Paul's request.

Previously overlooked details jumped out at him.

Onesimus has been of little use to you in the past, but now he is extremely useful to both of us.

Paul was correct. Onesimus had often been disobedient and lazy. He had spent more time in punishment than carrying out his functions. Had he changed?

He must have, because the man Paul described was not the slave he'd known.

If he has wronged you, charge it to me. Whatever he owes you, I'll repay.

Paul would cover the man's debt? Unbelievable! Did Paul know how much Onesimus owed him?

Still, the idea Paul would cover the debt incurred by a slave said a lot. Why would he do that?

Show kindness to my son. I became Onesimus' father in the faith while I was in prison.

I'm sending my son to you. Receive him with compassion.

Impossible! He threw out a hand. He'd be the laughingstock of his peers. Runaway slaves weren't accepted without punishment. And one certainly didn't treat them like honored guests or favored relatives.

His conscience pricked him again. God had forgiven him. Couldn't he find it in his heart to forgive Onesimus?

* * *

We don't know how the story ends, but we can hope it ended with Philemon forgiving Onesimus, accepting him back into his household, and treating him as a brother in Christ.

Paul certainly seemed confident that Philemon would be forgiving (Philemon 1:21).

The story of Philemon and Onesimus parallels our relationship with God.

God created us. He placed humanity on the Earth that He created and provided us with the resources. He gave us His Law and asked us to obey them.

But we turned our backs on Him. We decided we'd rather do as we pleased, regardless of the consequences or how our actions hurt God. We became slaves to sin, with no way to free ourselves or to pay our debts.

Jesus took our place on the cross. He used His blood to cover our debt. We didn't ask Him to. It was a gift that He offered freely.

Jesus wiped away our debts, so why do we find it difficult to do the same for others?

In His sermon on the Mount, Jesus taught His disciples that forgiveness was a crucial tenet of our relationship with God.

> *Matthew 6:14-15 NKJV — "For if you forgive men their trespasses, your heavenly Father will also forgive you.*
> *"But if you do not forgive men their trespasses, neither will your Father forgive your trespasses."*

This is an important lesson on the quest for forgiveness: we cancel the debts of those who have wronged us, even if they never ask us for forgiveness. We do it because this is what God, through Christ, did for us.

Prayer

Abba Father,

Forgiveness is hard, yet You ask it of me. Soften my heart and teach me to offer grace and forgiveness, even when I don't want to.

When it's difficult to forgive, remind me of Christ's sacrifice on the cross for my sins. In Jesus' name, Amen.

Go Deeper

Read Philemon.

- Imagine yourself in the wealthy slave owner's position. Do you believe Paul's request was reasonable? Explain the reasons for your answer.
- How can you apply the lessons of Philemon and Onesimus to your life?

Key Points

1. Onesimus was a runaway slave who became a Christian in the early church.
2. Paul sent Onesimus back to his owner and requested that he forgive him, restore his position, and treat him as a brother.
3. Forgiveness sometimes elevates us to a greater position

than we previously held.

18

Forgive Your Accusers

Matthew 5:44 NKJV — "But I say to you, love your enemies, bless those who curse you, do good to those who hate you, and pray for those who spitefully use you and persecute you,"

Stephen stood in the center of the large hall filled with leaders who would pass judgment on him. The spot between his shoulder blades twitched because of the crowd's hostile focus.

The judge looked down his nose at Stephen. "What crime has this man committed?"

Two thin men Stephen had never seen before came forward.

"We heard Stephen speak blasphemous words against Moses and God."

More witnesses testified, "He never stops speaking against this holy place and the Law.

"He said Jesus of Nazareth will destroy this place and change the customs Moses passed down to us."

The entire council bristled and glared at him.

The high priest narrowed his eyes at Stephen, "Are these accusa-

tions true?"

His heart pounded, and he swallowed the lump in his throat, determined to defend himself.

"My friends, listen to me! The God of glory appeared to our father Abraham while he was still in Mesopotamia before he lived in Harran."

He recounted the history of his people, taking comfort in the familiar narrative.

"When the time for God to fulfill His promise to Abraham drew near, the number of our people in Egypt had greatly increased."

God's timing never failed to amaze him. Didn't it mean then that he was meant to be at this place at this time, speaking to these men?

He drew in a breath, sending up a silent prayer for God to give him the right words.

"Moses was born, and he was no ordinary child."

The men nodded in agreement. Moses was their prophet, a great leader among our people.

He spoke about Moses's life in Pharaoh's house and in the Wilderness. The great man had walked with God his entire life.

Righteous indignation for his people's disregard for the God they professed to serve flooded his chest and he curled his fists.

"You stiff-necked people! Your hearts and ears are uncircumcised, and you're just like your ancestors. Always resisting the Holy Spirit! You murdered the Righteous One."

The men growled at him, the whole council surging toward him. Rough hands grabbed him, dragging him from the room. Stephen closed his eyes against the dizzying sensation and began to pray.

When he opened his eyes, he was in the town square, the council surrounding him. Gone were their dignified, aloof expressions, replaced with hate and anger.

They grabbed stones, throwing them at him. The projectiles thudded against him, bruising his skin and shattering bones. He gasped with pain but continued to pray for his attackers.

"Lord Jesus, receive my spirit." A sharp pain shot through him as his shin snapped and Stephen fell on his knees. "Lord, don't hold this sin against them."

* * *

Stephen's final words to his persecutors echoed Jesus' statement on the cross.

How could Stephen forgive the men who killed him? Christ had predicted what happened to Stephen.

> *Matthew 10:17-20 KJV — But beware of men: for they will deliver you up to the councils, and they will scourge you in their synagogues;*
>
> *And ye shall be brought before governors and kings for my sake, for a testimony against them and the Gentiles.*
>
> *But when they deliver you up, take no thought how or what ye shall speak: for it shall be given you in that same hour what ye shall speak.*
>
> *For it is not ye that speak, but the Spirit of your Father which speaketh in you.*

Perhaps Stephen was encouraged during his trial when he remembered God's faithfulness.

When he saw the vision of Jesus standing at the right hand of God, maybe he recalled His promise to prepare mansions in heaven.

My friend, forgiveness is not easy. Yet God asks it of us anyway. Let us emulate Stephen and Jesus, forgiving even when it hurts.

Prayer

Dear heavenly Father,

Persecution is never easy, but is guaranteed for those who follow You. Lord, I want to be Your witness, a beacon of hope to other believers.

Help me remain faithful when I am tested for my faith. In Jesus' name, Amen.

Go Deeper

Read Acts 6–7

- Imagine yourself in Stephen's position. What emotions might he have experienced?
- How do you relate to him?
- What lessons from Stephen can you model in your life?

Key Points

1. The scribes and Pharisees accused Stephen of blaspheming against Moses and God so they had an excuse to execute him.
2. Stephen defended himself—and Christ—by recounting Israel's history, chastising them for not acknowledging the Messiah.
3. You may be called to defend your beliefs before a hostile

group. Remain faithful as the Holy Spirit will help you.

19

Forgive Those Who Persecute You

James 5:16 NLT — Confess your sins to each other and pray for each other so that you may be healed. The earnest prayer of a righteous person has great power and produces wonderful results.

"**Y**ou believe in Jesus and want to be one of His disciples?" *Skepticism coated Barnabas's question as he hovered at the door of Saul's sitting room, wariness and disbelief dancing over his features.*

Saul didn't blame the man. A short time ago, he'd persecuted anyone who professed to believe in Jesus. He imprisoned many believers and had stood and watched as they stoned Stephen to death.

"Yes." Shame for everything he'd done to make the believers uncomfortable threatened to crush him under its weight.

But if he didn't convince at least one of Jesus' followers that he was sincere, how would they learn they had nothing to fear from him?

"Why?" Barnabas scowled at him. "Why should we believe this isn't a trick? A way for you to infiltrate the church to get more details

about our members?"

Saul sighed. "I don't expect you to believe me." He'd had some version of this conversation with several of the disciples.

Barnabas crossed his arms over his chest. "Convince me."

Saul took the arched eyebrow as a challenge and began his story.

"It started after Stephen's death." If he closed his eyes, he could still picture the scene. "I was determined to imprison everyone who believes in Jesus. I asked the high priest for letters to the synagogues in Damascus.

"My plan was to take anyone who belonged to the Way, male or female, as prisoners to Jerusalem."

Barnabas scoffed. "Tell me something I don't know."

"As I neared Damascus, a light from heaven flashed around me. I fell to the ground, and a voice spoke, 'Saul, Saul, why do you persecute me?'

"There was so much power in the voice that I trembled. 'Who are you, Lord?' I asked.

"'I am Jesus, whom you are persecuting' the Voice replied. 'Get up and go into the city, and you will be told what to do.'"

Barnabas crept closer, as if drawn by Saul's narrative. "What happened next?"

"When I got up from the ground, I was blind and had to be led by the men who were with me. I remained blind for three days, and didn't eat or drink anything during that entire time.

"On the third day, a man named Ananias visited me. He said Jesus had sent him. After he rested his hands on my eyes, my sight returned."

Barnabas sank onto the couch, wonderment on his face. "You had an encounter with Jesus."

Yes," Saul admitted. "I don't know why God forgave me after the way I persecuted His people, but I will spend the rest of my life telling everyone about my experience. I want everyone to know Jesus is the Son of God."

* * *

Saul's Damascus experience had a powerful impact on him. He changed from a man persecuting the Christians to a leader of the early church.

Thirteen of the twenty-seven books of the New Testament were written by Paul (Saul) the Apostle. Not bad for a man who once wanted nothing to do with followers of "The Way".

Not every Christian began their journey believing in God, but their experience affects them in two ways.

1. They give a stronger testimony about what they believe and why. As Jesus said to Simon the Pharisee, the person who has been forgiven much loves more than the person who was forgiven little.
2. It is a testament to God's grace and ability to forgive those who transgress against Him. We can do nothing to earn God's forgiveness, which He freely bestows on anyone who asks.

God's grace reveals His marvelous character. It reminds us He is our Creator and heavenly Father. He loves us and wants nothing more than to welcome us into His presence, and later into His kingdom.

Do not disregard the treasure of God's forgiveness.

Prayer

Dear heavenly Father,

Forgive me, for I have sinned against You. Thanks for the grace that pardons me every time I ask. Please don't let me take it for granted.

May I always remember that Your grace is greater than my sins and seek forgiveness for them. In Jesus's name, Amen.

Go Deeper

Read Acts 9

- How do you think Saul felt during his encounter with Jesus and the subsequent days?
- Were the disciples wrong to not immediately accept him? Why do you believe they held back?
- What lessons can you learn from Saul's experience and how will you implement them?

Key Points

1. Jesus appeared to Paul on his way to Damascus. This experience changed Paul and had a lingering impact on Christianity.
2. Paul became a stalwart force in the church, writing almost fifty percent of the New Testament books.
3. An encounter with Christ changes us, leaving us different

from who we were before.

20

Forgiveness Reunites You With God

2 Corinthians 5:17 NLT — This means that anyone who belongs to Christ has become a new person. The old life is gone; a new life has begun!

*B*enesh trudged along behind the Man they called 'Messiah'. They had done such a number on Him, the Man couldn't carry His cross. He stumbled for the umpteenth time, halting the procession.

Benesh hitched his cross higher on his shoulder, the wood scraping against his cheek while more splinters pierced the flesh of his palm. He wouldn't complain. This was as he deserved. He'd defied Roman law and now must pay the price.

"You there!" A soldier seized a Cyrenian and hauled him toward the fallen Man. "Carry His cross."

The Cyrenian didn't protest. The Romans could be brutal—better to carry someone's cross for a few miles than to be hung on one.

He grimaced at his dark humor. How had he gotten to this place? Thank heavens his mother wasn't alive to see what he'd become. Benesh switched his attention back to the Man.

The crowds followed along, shouting and deriding Him. That was unusual. Crucifixions were Rome's way of exerting their dominance.

They stuck terror in the people's hearts, quelling uprisings and rebellion. They did not attract crowds of people reveling in the act.

What had this Man done to earn the ire of the scribes and Pharisees, the men jeering the loudest?

And why were there so many among the crowd who stared at the Man as if their hopes had been crushed?

His thoughts distracted him long enough for him and his two companions to be hung. They had placed the Man in the center— one criminal on either side. Benesh didn't run in the same company as Lior, but he'd heard of him. The man was unparalleled in his defiance of Rome.

From the cross, Benesh had a clear view of the masses below. People stretched for miles, as far as the eye could see.

Many faced the Man in the middle, their expressions scornful. Snippets of conversation drifted up to him.

"You who claimed You would destroy the temple and rebuild it in three days, save Yourself! If You are the Son of God, come down from the cross."

Benesh's gaze fell on the soldiers at the foot of the cross. The men ignored the crowds as they cast lots for the Man's clothing. Why would they want the discarded robes of a criminal?

Whatever. Benesh scoffed. Who understood why the Romans did anything?

He tuned into the crowd's mockery of the Man beside him.

"He saved others but cannot save Himself. If He is the King of Israel, let Him come down from the cross, and we will believe Him."

"He trusted in God; let His Father deliver Him if He will have Him; for He said, 'I am the Son of God.'"

Benesh turned to the Man with a sneer. "You're the Son of God?"

He laughed derisively, Lior joining in.

Benesh insulted the Man they called the Messiah, his loud voice blending with Lior's and the crowd's. It distracted him from the pain of balancing his torn and ravaged flesh on two metal spikes.

Clouds rolled across the sky and Benesh stared up at them. Would it rain? No. Something about these clouds felt different. Almost as if the Earth mourned today's event. He scoffed at the fanciful thought. Death was making him a poet.

They part my garments among them, and cast lots upon my vesture.

A long-forgotten Scripture, memorized at his father's knee, drifted through Benesh's mind.

He is despised and rejected of men; a man of sorrows, and acquainted with grief: and we hid as it were our faces from him; he was despised, and we esteemed him not.

Benesh rolled his head to stare at the Man. What if He was the Messiah, and this was a fulfillment of the ancient prophecies?

Oh, dear Lord, is this Your Son?

Shame for how he'd reviled the Man rolled through him.

"If You are the Christ," Lior began in a derisive tone, "save Yourself and us."

No! Did the man not realize what he was doing? It was blasphemy. Plain and simple.

Benesh narrowed his eyes at Lior. "Don't you fear God, seeing you are under the same condemnation? We receive the due reward of our deeds, but this Man has done nothing wrong."

The conviction that he spoke the truth brought the first glimmer of peace since his arrest.

Benesh spoke to the Messiah, "Lord, remember me when You come into Your kingdom."

"Assuredly, I say to you today," the Messiah replied, "you will be

with Me in Paradise."

Peace settled in Benesh's spirit. Had he ever met such a Man? One who brought hope at the darkest hour of his life?

Dear Lord, please forgive me for my sins.

* * *

The thief on the cross started out taunting Christ, but had an epiphany and sought mercy instead.

Jesus graciously forgave the man and promised him a place in paradise.

My friend, God wants to forgive His children and offer them a place in the new world. Even if repentance comes at the last minute, God's forgiveness is instantaneous.

But I caution you against waiting to seek forgiveness. None of us know the hour of our deaths or if we'll be cognizant when the moment arises. Do not delay repentance and turning to God.

My friend, if you hear God's voice, please don't harden your heart.

Prayer

Dear heavenly Father,

Like the thief on the cross, I'm unworthy of Your forgiveness. Thanks for keeping Your promise and not treating me as my sins deserve.

Forgive me for every transgression. In Jesus' name, Amen.

Go Deeper

Read Matthew 27:38-44 and Luke 23:39-43

- Why do you think one thief went from reviling Jesus to defending Him?
- What do you learn from the thieves crucified with Christ?
- What lessons from this account might you want to share with future generations?

Key Points

1. At Jesus' crucifixion, both thieves taunted Him. However, before His death, one thief recognized who Jesus was and sought forgiveness.
2. Even if you repent in the last moments of your life, God is ready to forgive.
3. Don't wait until the last minute to seek forgiveness.

21

Jesus Forgives Your Sins

John 3:17 NKJV — "For God did not send His Son into the world to condemn the world, but that the world through Him might be saved."

*T*he scribes and Pharisees infiltrated the crowd while Jesus taught in the temple.

Here we go again, Father. Why can't the teachers of Your people understand what I'm saying?

He braced Himself for their attack. His time was running out. Soon, He wouldn't be here to preach and teach.

"By what authority are You doing these things?" they asked.

"I will also ask you one question," Jesus replied. "If you answer Me, I'll tell you by who gave Me the authority to do these things. Where did John's baptism come from—heaven or earth?"

They debated among themselves.

"We don't know," they finally answered.

"Neither will I tell you by what authority I'm doing these things." Jesus returned His attention to the crowd, His heart clenching with compassion.

They were so lost. He launched into a parable about a man with two sons, hoping they'd see the comparison.

"Hear another parable: There was a certain householder, which planted a vineyard, and hedged it round about, and dug a winepress in it, and built a tower, and let it out to husbandmen, and went into a far country.

"And when the time of the fruit drew near, he sent his servants to the husbandmen, that they might receive their portion."

The landowner's request was within his rights. Because it was his land, he could demand up to fifty percent of the harvest.

"And the husbandmen took his servants, and beat one, and killed another, and stoned another."

Jesus mourned for the prophets the Israelites had abused and killed because they spoke the truth to people who didn't want to hear.

"Again, he sent other servants, and they treated them the same. Finally, he sent his son, saying, 'They will reverence my son.'

"But when the husbandmen saw the son, they said among themselves, 'This is the heir; come, let us kill him, and let us seize on his inheritance.'

"And they caught him, and cast him out of the vineyard, and killed him."

Tears pricked Jesus' eyes. He was the Son. He would be further mistreated and crucified, all because the children of Israel refused to accept the truth.

Father, forgive them, for they don't understand the depths of their transgressions.

* * *

The Bible is a story of God's love for humanity, man's rejection of that love, and God's continued forgiveness.

God chose the Israelites as His special people. They had no unique traits, but He loved them.

Israel was to obey God's commandments and be an example to the world, drawing men to worship God.

Sadly, they abused their exalted position as God's chosen people. They turned their backs on Him, worshipped idols, and mistreated His prophets.

Yet the Lord continued to reach out to His recalcitrant people, reminding them of His love, warning of the coming judgment, and exhorting them to return to Him.

When Jesus came to Earth, He had full knowledge that they would mistreat Him, and He would die for the sins of the entire world.

My friend, God wants to forgive us and sent His Son to die for us. If you have unconfessed sin, do not waste another minute. Cry out to God and ask for His forgiveness. He is waiting to hear from you.

Prayer

Dear heavenly Father,

Forgive me, for I have sinned. I don't always do what is right and sometimes find it easier to do wrong.

Help me hide Your Word in my heart so I won't sin against You. Lead me on the right path, so I won't deviate from Your will.

Take my life, Lord, and consecrate it. I surrender my will to You. In Jesus' name, Amen.

Go Deeper

Read Matthew 21:33–41 and Matthew 27

- How do you think Jesus felt as He told the parable of the vineyard?
- What parallels do you see between Jesus' life and ministry to parable of the landowner's son?
- What does this passage teach you about God and how can you incorporate the lessons?

Key Points

1. The parable of the winepress is a metaphor for God's relationship with the children of Israel.
2. Even after the Israelites' disobedience, Jesus died for their sins.
3. Jesus gave up heaven to die for you. Don't disregard His sacrifice.

II

Additional Resources

22

How to Forgive and Move On

As sinful human beings, we crave God's forgiveness, but sometimes find it difficult to forgive others. So how do we learn to forgive and move on?

What Does It Mean To Forgive?

When we are in pain or angry, we often want to make the person who hurt us feel the same way we do. We plot our revenge or dream of ways to make them pay for what they did. We may cut that person out of our lives.

When we forgive, we cancel the debt ascribed to their account. We make a deliberate choice[1] to release our hurt, anguish, anger, and thoughts of vengeance toward that person.

---

[1] For additional information on the impact of our choices, read Adam & Eve: Our Choices Matter https://hebrews12endurance.com/adam-and-eve/

Learning How to Forgive and Move On

Westerners are taught to "forgive and forget" until we believe that forgetting is synonymous with forgiveness.

But forgiveness is a choice—one we may have to make many times before it sticks. We must *choose* to let go of our anger, pain, and our thoughts of vengeance. We choose to forgive and move on with our lives.

What the Bible Says About Forgiveness

As we learn how to forgive, we need to spend time in the Word, reading and memorizing verses about forgiveness. Here are a few verses to get you started:

> *Ephesians 4:32 KJV — And be ye kind one to another, tenderhearted, forgiving one another, even as God for Christ's sake hath forgiven you.*

> *Mark 11:25 KJV — And when ye stand praying, forgive, if ye have ought against any: that your Father also which is in heaven may forgive you your trespasses.*

> *Matthew 6:15 KJV — But if you do not forgive others their trespasses, neither will your Father forgive your trespasses.*

> *Matthew 18:21-22 KJV — Then came Peter to him, and said, Lord, how oft shall my brother sin against me, and I forgive him? till seven times?*
>
> *Jesus saith unto him, I say not unto thee, Until seven*

times: but, Until seventy times seven.

Colossians 3:13 KJV — Forbearing one another, and forgiving one another, if any man have a quarrel against any: even as Christ forgave you, so also do ye.

Proverbs 10:12 KJV — Hatred stirreth up strifes: but love covereth all sins.

1 Corinthians 10:13 KJV — There hath no temptation taken you but such as is common to man: but God is faithful, who will not suffer you to be tempted above that ye are able; but will with the temptation also make a way to escape, that ye may be able to bear it.

Romans 12:17 KJV — Recompense to no man evil for evil. Provide things honest in the sight of all men.

1 Peter 3:9 KJV — Not rendering evil for evil, or railing for railing: but contrariwise blessing; knowing that ye are thereunto called, that ye should inherit a blessing.

How to Forgive and Move On

The Bible has a lot to say about forgiveness, even saying if we refuse to forgive others, our Father will not forgive us of our sins (Matthew 6:15).

Because we know the benefits of God's forgiveness, we must decide to forgive others so we can remain in our Father's presence[2].

---

[2] This was first published on November 24, 2019 on Hebrews12Endurance.com https://hebrews12endurance.com/how-to-forgive-and-move-on/

23

3 Amazing Benefits of God's Forgiveness

Sometimes we take forgiveness for granted. We assume that because we're Christians, God's forgiveness is automatic. It's not, and we need to remind ourselves that it's important for us to ask for it.

Why We Need Forgiveness

God created a perfect couple and gave them one rule which they broke, and sin entered the world. Sin puts a barrier between us and God, one we cannot cross on our own.

Forgiveness lowers the wall between us and God and allows us to stand in His presence again. It restores our ability to commune with Him. We need God's forgiveness to restore our relationship. Without forgiveness, we remain separated from God, unable to enter His presence.

How to Receive Forgiveness from God

To receive God's forgiveness, we must ask for it. The Bible tells us that if we confess our sins, God is just and will forgive us and cleanse us from all unrighteousness (1 John 1:9).

When we confess our sins with a contrite heart and humble spirit, God forgives us and removes every trace of unrighteousness from us. He imbues us with the righteousness of His Son Jesus and labels us holy.

Forgiveness is a gift from God. It is not our right or something we're due. It's a gift because He loves us and not because we deserve it.

How God's Forgiveness Benefits Us

1. God's forgiveness allows us to forgive others. Let's face it: forgiveness is hard...especially when the person who hurt us refuses to acknowledge what they did or apologize. Our inability to forgive becomes even more difficult if they continue to hurt us.

Yet, if we remember how God forgives us even though we don't deserve it, we can apply that same grace to people who hurt us or let us down.

2. Accepting God's forgiveness allows us to forgive ourselves. Sometimes the vilest sinner we know looks at us in the mirror. We remember our sins and evil deeds and believe God can't forgive us. We limit God's ability to forgive. Thank God He doesn't accept our puny limits.

Isaiah 1:18 KJV — "Come now, and let us reason together,

saith the Lord: though your sins be as scarlet, they shall be as white as snow; though they be red like crimson, they shall be as wool."

Our sins may be the worst crimes ever conceptualized in human imaginations, but God's grace and forgiveness are enough to make them as white as snow—newly fallen snow–unmarred by any tint, film, or dirt—snow so white it hurts the eyes to look at.

3. God's forgiveness allows us to live free. Living with the guilt and shame of sin becomes a burden felt in every area of life.

Sin's shackles imprison us, preventing us from truly living. When we live outside of God's forgiveness, the enemy attacks us with ferocity because he wants us to feel defeated. He wants us to believe God can't forgive us because our sins are too dark.

But when we repent, confess our sins, and accept God's forgiveness, a weight lifts from our shoulders and we experience the peace Jesus promised.

John 14:27 NKJV — Peace I leave with you, My peace I give to you; not as the world gives do I give to you. Let not your heart be troubled, neither let it be afraid.

We become new creatures, basking in God's forgiveness and grace[3].

---

[3] This was first published on Hebrews12Endurance.com September 19, 2019 https://hebrews12endurance.com/benefits-of-gods-forgiveness/

24

6 Fascinating Characteristics of God's Grace

As Christians, we love to talk about God's grace. One of our favorite quotes is, 'We're saved by grace', which is an awesome truth but, do we understand the depth of God's grace?

What is Meant by God's Grace?

I don't know how it is where you live, but in Jamaica, many Christians believe God's grace originated with Jesus' birth. But if we're to understand God's grace, we must return to the Garden of Eden and the moment Eve believed the enemy's lies and ate the forbidden fruit.

When Eve realized her eyes were open, she gave the fruit to Adam, and he also ate. Both disobeyed God's Law, for which the punishment, as they had been told, would be death. Had it not been for God's grace, that would have been the end of humanity.

Let's be honest here, it would have been easy for God to destroy Adam and Eve and start over with two perfect people, but He didn't. He put the plan of salvation in place,

> Genesis 3:15 NLT — *"And I will cause hostility between you and the woman, and between your offspring and her offspring. He will strike your head, and you will strike his heel."*

Definitions of Grace

The Merriam-Webster Dictionary defines grace as "unmerited divine assistance given to humans for their regeneration or sanctification."

This definition is wordy, so let's put it this way: God's grace is the undeserved kindness extended toward humanity.

The word typically translated as grace in the New Testament is the Greek cháris[4], (pronounced khar'-ece). Cháris refers to the divine influence upon the heart, and its reflection in the life; including gratitude.

It could also have been translated to mean benefit, favor, or gift. According to the Blue Letter Bible, the typical usage of the word cháris was:

> "of the merciful kindness by which God, exerting his holy influence upon souls, turns them to Christ, keeps, strengthens, increases them in Christian faith, knowledge, affection, and kindles them to the exercise of the Christian virtues."

---

4 "H3068 - Y³hōvâ - Strong's Hebrew Lexicon (kjv)." Blue Letter Bible. Accessed 27 Dec, 2024. https://www.blueletterbible.org/lexicon/h3068/kjv/wlc/0-1/

God lavishes us with His grace and it exerts an influence on us that draws us to Christ, who saves us.

If you think about it for a second, you'll realize that everyone is a recipient of God's grace. It is because of God's grace that anyone is still alive today.

The Bible says all have sinned and come short of God's glory (Romans 3:23). Jesus Christ is the only person who obeyed God without sin.

What the Bible Says About God's Grace

The Bible has a lot to say about grace. Even when the word is not used, we see evidence of God treating people with kindness and favor. Let's look at a few verses on God's grace and see what lessons we can learn.

1. Grace is a gift.

God freely lavishes His grace on us. We can't earn it, but He gives it anyway. God's grace isn't dependent on our good behavior, status, moral standing, or anything we do. It's God's gift because He loves us.

Ephesians 2:8-9 KJV — For by grace are ye saved through faith; and that not of yourselves: it is the gift of God:
Not of works, lest any man should boast.

2. Grace brings salvation.

When Christ died on the cross, it became the doorway to salvation for those who would believe. Our works do not lead to salvation. We receive it through the blood of Jesus[5] and is freely accessible to everyone.

> *Romans 5:8 KJV — But God commendeth his love toward us, in that, while we were yet sinners, Christ died for us.*

3. God's grace allows us to live godly lives.

It's one thing to be saved by the grace of God. It's another for us to continue the work necessary for our sanctification. When you accept Jesus as your Lord and Savior, the journey is just beginning.

You must put off your carnal self and strive towards holiness. I'm sure you know by now that the carnal man is strong! But he's no match for God. It's the Holy Spirit who accomplishes this work of sanctification by working in us and through us.

> *Titus 2:11-14 KJV — For the grace of God that bringeth salvation hath appeared to all men,*
> *Teaching us that, denying ungodliness and worldly lusts, we should live soberly, righteously, and godly, in this present world;*
> *Looking for that blessed hope, and the glorious appearing of the great God and our Saviour Jesus Christ;*

---

[5] To further explore Jesus' work on the cross, read The True Meaning of the Cross of Jesus https://hebrews12endurance.com/thankful-for-the-cross/

> *Who gave himself for us, that he might redeem us from all iniquity, and purify unto himself a peculiar people, zealous of good works.*

4. God's grace is patient.

Many people died believing Jesus would have returned in their lifetime, and I'm pretty sure every generation thinks they're living in the last days. Yet the world continues to turn as God tarries. Why?

It's because God wants to save as many people as possible. If it were up to Him, nobody would be lost and so He extends His grace towards humanity, hoping we'll learn to love, honor, and worship Him as He deserves.

> *2 Peter 3:9 KJV — The Lord is not slack concerning his promise, as some men count slackness; but is longsuffering to us-ward, not willing that any should perish, but that all should come to repentance.*

5. Everyone has received grace.

We only need to consider the condition of our world to know that everyone has received grace. We breathe in the air God has created; we eat the food He provides, and His rains benefit all people (Matthew 5:25).

> *Ephesians 4:7 KJV — But unto every one of us is given grace according to the measure of the gift of Christ.*

6. We can't "out-sin" God's grace.

The devil sometimes deceives us by claiming our sins are too great to be forgiven. But God's grace has no measure.

> *Romans 5:20 KJV — Moreover the law entered, that the offence might abound. But where sin abounded, grace did much more abound:*

As you ponder the meaning of grace, I encourage you to read through a list of verses on what the Bible says about grace[6]. Find them in your Bibles and underline them. Or print them out and keep them for when you need a reminder of God's grace.

Benefits of God's Grace

God's grace gives us the power to fight our battles against the enemy. It empowers us to forgive those who hurt us. It strengthens us in our faith and teaches us how to live in a way that honors God and brings glory to His name.

As God's grace works in our hearts, we learn how to extend it to others. Through our actions, grace blesses those who come in contact with us and becomes a testimony to those who want to serve God[7].

---

[6] For a comprehensive list on grace, read through this collection: https://www.openbible.info/topics/grace

[7] This was first published April 11, 2021 on Hebrews12Endurance.com https://hebrews12endurance.com/grace/

25

10 Practical Steps to Forget the Past

Are you doing things you know are wrong because of something that happened in the past? You may need to forget the past.

It may not seem possible, but it's necessary if you're going to step into your God-given identity.

What Does It Mean to Forget the Past?

We are the sum of our experiences–good, bad, and indifferent, so under what circumstances should we strive to forget the past?

Before we get into that, let me explain what I mean by 'forgetting the past'. This may be impossible, depending on how good your memory is, especially if the event was significant.

The more significant events in our past are often harmful ones. They may involve abuse, pain, neglect or other things we truly wish we had never experienced. Because of our experiences, we may become distrustful, standoffish, or hurtful.

To move beyond the pain, we must learn to forget the past. Please do not take this information as a substitute for professional help if required.

That being said, sometimes we need to employ the forgetfulness God does when dealing with our forgiven sin. We know God doesn't forget, but when we repent and ask for forgiveness, He treats us as if we had never sinned.

In order to move forward, we need to make peace with the past so it doesn't destroy our futures.

10 Tips to Make Peace with Your Past Biblically

1. **Admit that the pain exists.** A common reaction to pain is to pretend it doesn't exist. We bury our heads in the proverbial sand, to get past our wounded selves. But an untreated wound doesn't heal, it festers.

Admitting the pain gives us room to seek help for it.

2. **Express your pain.** This may seem similar to the previous step, but it's not. After admitting that your pain exists, it needs a safe outlet for expression. The last thing you want to do is hurt someone because you don't know what to do with your pain.

Journaling, exercise, art, and other creative pursuits are great ways to express your pain. Find a creative outlet, don't let your pain consume you.

3. **Get support or professional help where necessary.** Sometimes processing our trauma requires professional help. Seek reputable counselors who can guide you in ways that align with the Bible and what God says about you.

4. **Capture your thoughts.** We have many random, negative thoughts daily. You probably already know that. But you may

not realize how often you have the same random, negative thoughts.

If you were to pay attention to what you think about every day, it might surprise you how often the same thought wanders through your mind. What's worse is that it conjures up the same emotions every time.

Maybe that's why the apostle Paul said we should capture every thought and subject them to the law of Christ.

Pay attention to your thoughts and put them through the Philippians 4:8 test. Ask yourself, is the thought:

- True?
- Noble?
- Pure?
- Right?
- Lovely?
- Excellent?
- Praiseworthy?

If it meets the criteria, great. If it doesn't, hold it up to the Word of God. What hidden lie does it contain and how can you banish it with truth?

5. **Identify where you allow past scripts to direct your present.** Like our thoughts, our behavior follows a pattern. One incentive for forgetting the past is that old ways of thinking and responding affect your present.

Examine your behavior and figure out if you're responding from a place of old pain.

6. **Forgive yourself and any others involved.** Is there someone

you need to forgive? You've probably heard it before, but unforgiveness only hurts you. Many times, the person we haven't forgiven isn't aware of how we feel about them or they don't care.

Do the work needed to forgive them, and yourself, so you can forget the past.

7. **Look for God's fingerprint. One lie the** enemy uses with people repeatedly is that God has abandoned or forgotten us. I know. It's a lie he's told me many times and I'm sure he's told you the same. But we don't have to believe him.

Instead, we can choose to look for God's hand in our story. I'm sure when you look at what you've been through, you'll see God protecting you, caring for you, and sending people to do the same.

8. **Identify the dominant lie.** Is there something connected to your past pain you repeat often? Is it true?

The lies we believe permeate every area of our lives...even our relationship with God. Spend time in prayer and ask God to reveal the lies you believe so you can put them behind you.

9. **Replace the lie with Truth.** Okay, now you've figured out the lie (or lies) you believe. It's time to replace the lies[8] of the enemy with the truth of your Heavenly Father.

Do a Bible study on what God says about you and meditate on the truth of the Word.

---

[8] For more on how to replace the devil's lies with truth, read 13 Inspiring Verses When You Feel Not Good Enough https://hebrews12endurance.com/enough-sharon-jaynes-review/

10. **Reinforce your future identity with Scripture**. You've dealt with the pain of your past and identified the lies that threaten to destroy your present. Now you need to safeguard the future.

The enemy is good at reminding us of our mistakes like they are still happening. We will not let him continue to do that. Let us reinforce our identity in Christ by focusing on who we want to become.

Let me explain what I mean. Galatians 5 talks about the difference between living in the spirit and in the flesh. Paul lists several things experienced by people who live in the flesh: adultery, fornication, uncleanness, lasciviousness, and so on (Galatians 5:19–21).

But he also talked about the fruit of the spirit: love, joy, peace, longsuffering, gentleness, goodness, faith, meekness, temperance (Galatians 5:22–23).

As we learn to embody our identities in Christ, let us focus on our future selves. Pray for the fruit of the Spirit. Ask God to imbue you with the Holy Spirit and invite Him to live out His life through you. Find Scriptures that empower you to overcome the fears and challenges of your past.

You Are Not Your Past

You may have done something you wish you could obliterate from your history. Or worse, you had an experience that changed the way you see yourself and colored your choices since.

Let me remind you of an important lesson: you are not your past. Forgetting your past may be the key to embracing your identity in Christ[9].

Those are hard words to internalize because the enemy enjoys reminding us of what we want to forget. He likes to tell us we're not enough or that we'll never get over that thing we want to forget. But he lies.

He was a liar from the beginning and he's lying now.

When we accept Christ as our Lord and Savior, He takes us, washes the gunk away, and makes us clean. Then He covers us in righteous robes and makes us new. We can walk away from our mistakes because we are not our past.

Your Past Is Not Your Future

This is another lie the enemy wants us to believe: our future will look exactly like our past. Oh, sweet friend, that's only true if you listen to him. But I encourage you, don't fall for the devil's lies. Don't let him tell you the dark plans he has for you.

Instead, choose to listen to your heavenly Father and root your identity in Him. Don't allow the things you did in the past to define who you are. You don't have to keep doing them if you don't want to. If you ask, God will give you the victory over the sin that keeps dragging you under.

I know it's hard to believe because sometimes I struggle with it, but things won't always be as dismal as they look now.

But if you're going to get to the future God has in store for you, stop doing the devil's work for him. Remember: you are

---

[9] For a crash course in your identity in Christ, check out this Bible study Our Identity in Christ Bible Study https://hebrews12endurance.com/identity-i n-christ/

not your past and your past is not your future[10].

---

[10] This was first published on Hebrews12Endurance.com on April 30, 2021 https://hebrews12endurance.com/you-are-not-your-past/

26

Conclusion

Thank you for taking this journey with me as we examined 21 stories on forgiveness and picked several reminders and tips.

Though the enemy tries to convince us otherwise, God is ready to forgive us if we come to Him with a repentant and contrite heart.

When someone betrays us, it might seem impossible to forgive them. But if we're willing to sit with God and wrestle with our unforgiveness, He'll give us peace.

When we forgive others (or receive forgiveness), it transforms our lives, lifting us from the ashes of our past and setting us on the path leading to the bright future God has in store for us.

One of the major lessons we learned is that after God forgives us, there might still be consequences. We may need to make restitution. But the key, as we move on, is to live forgiven. Don't let the enemy—or yourself—keep you trapped in the mire of your past when God has forgiven you.

If you enjoyed this devotional, I'd appreciate it if you'd leave a review online and share it with your friends.

For a supplementary resource on new beginnings, join my newsletter for the mini-ebook: A Fresh Start: https://BookHip.com/PZLVFDF.

Please also check out *His Perfect Wife*, the novel that inspired this devotional.

27

His Perfect Wife

He shattered her heart once. Can she trust him to make it whole again?

Tonya McPherson once believed she'd marry her first love. But when Malcolm Hall walked away four years ago, he took more than her dreams—he took her faith in love itself. Now, Tonya has moved on... or so she tells herself. But when Malcolm reappears as the new youth pastor at her church, she's faced with the one man she vowed to forget. Can her heart survive the onslaught of old memories and unresolved feelings?

Malcolm Hall knows he made the worst mistake of his life when he left Tonya. His return to Orange Valley isn't just about answering God's call—it's about making things right. But earning Tonya's forgiveness, and maybe even her love, is going to take more than an apology. It will take faith, patience, and a second chance neither of them is sure they deserve.

Can they let go of the pain of the past to embrace the love they were meant for? Or will fear and pride rob them of their happily ever after?

His Perfect Wife *is the heartwarming prequel to a Christian romance series set in Orange Valley—a tale of love, redemption, and God's perfect timing in every detail of our lives.*

About Aminata

Her passionate love affair with books began with an upside-down copy of Silas Marner, and she's dedicated her life to helping women understand the truth of the Bible for themselves.

She writes to point to a God bigger than our failings and provide hope to others. Aminata lives in Montego Bay, Jamaica with her husband and son.

Aminata Coote is also a Christian romance author. Some of her novels include *His Perfect Wife* and *A Husband for Christmas*.

Connect with her on her website, aminatacoote.com, or on Instagram or Facebook @aminatacoote.

Sign up for Aminata's newsletter at https://tinyurl.com/Face FearEbook and get a copy of the free e-book Face Your Fears.

Other Books by Aminata

Devotionals

How To Find Your Gratitude Attitude

Draw Closer 52-Week Devotional Journal

Praying Your Way Through Social Media: Reflections for Christian Artists and Entrepreneurs (collaboration with Latasha Strachan)

God Sees You: 21 Devotions for the Woman Who Feels Invisible

The Battle Is Not Yours: 21 Devotions for Spiritual Warfare

God Is In Control: 21 Devotions on God's Sovereignty

Forgive Them: 21 Devotions on Forgiveness

Christian Living

Face Your Fear: Choose Faith Over Fear

Affirmations for Christian Women: Biblical Affirmations for Spiritual and Emotional Self-Care

7 Lessons on Endurance from Hebrews 12:1-2

Through God's Eyes: Marriage Lessons for Women

Unwavering: How to Stand Strong in Your Faith

Bible Study Workbooks

The Book of Haggai Bible Study Workbook

Bible Study Workbook on the Book of Ezra

For Teens

Royal: Lessons from the Book of Esther

Inspirational Contemporary Romance

Orange Valley Series
His Perfect Wife
His Perfect Match
His Perfect Family
His Perfect Choice

Christmas with the Porters
A Husband for Christmas
A Family for Christmas
A Wife For Christmas
A Daughter for Christmas

Learn more about my books at https://tinyurl.com/ACooteBooks

www.ingramcontent.com/pod-product-compliance
Lightning Source LLC
Chambersburg PA
CBHW061537120726
48001CB00004B/1594